MIRACLE MOMENTS
IN
KANSAS CITY ROYALS
HISTORY

THE TURNING POINTS,
THE MEMORABLE GAMES,
THE INCREDIBLE RECORDS

By Jeff Deters

SPORTS PUBLISHING

Sports Publishing books may be purchased in bulk at special discounts for sales promotion, corporate gifts, fund-raising, or educational purposes. Special editions can also be created to specifications. For details, contact the Special Sales Department, Sports Publishing, 307 West 36th Street, 11th Floor, New York, NY 10018 or sportspubbooks@skyhorsepublishing.com.

Sports Publishing® is a registered trademark of Skyhorse Publishing, Inc.®, a Delaware corporation.

Visit our website at www.sportspubbooks.com.

10 9 8 7 6 5 4 3 2 1

Library of Congress Cataloging-in-Publication Data is available on file.

Cover design by Tom Lau
Cover photo credit: Associated Press

ISBN: 978-1-61321-995-9
Ebook ISBN: 978-1-61321-996-6

Printed in China

Contents

Part Four: A Royal Rebirth

Introduction

The glove didn't fit my hand. I was probably about eight or ten at the time, and while in the store, I said the brown Wilson glove fit fine. But it really wasn't much bigger than my left hand, so it was actually a tight squeeze from the moment I put it on. But I had to have that glove.

It certainly wasn't the most expensive glove in the store. If it was, there's no way it would have made it back to my house, and I certainly wouldn't be writing about it now. I'm not sure if it was even my first glove, but it's the only glove that I can remember being mine, so I think it was.

I remember playing baseball in the backyard for hours with my brothers and sister, catching pop flies, liners, and grounders. There were surely gloves that fit my hand better that day in the store, but this glove had George Brett's name on it, right in the palm of my hand.

Like many others back then, my dream as a young kid was to play third base for the Kansas City Royals. That obviously didn't happen. And at my age now, let's hope it never does. For years, I had a blue Royals jacket similar to the one Dick

Howser wore. I wore it plenty as a kid, and all these years later, it still brings back memories of a special time.

The story of the Royals franchise is one of success, failure, heartbreak, triumph, and hope. And I hope I illustrate that in the following pages of this book. In it you will read personal tales from people, players, coaches, and staff who helped make the Royals one of the most beloved teams in sports. You'll find a few of my own personal tales as they—surprisingly to me—also intertwine with Royals history at times.

The first Royals game I covered as a reporter was May 2, 2013, the Snow Game. As I drove north on I-435 on a wet, gloomy Thursday morning, I wasn't exactly sure what to expect once I got to the stadium. In the clubhouse, one of the first people I talked to was Fox Sports Kansas City broadcaster Joel Goldberg. Not long after that, I saw Rex Hudler greet fellow FSKC broadcaster and Royals Hall of Famer Jeff Montgomery with a chest bump. Yes, you really do see everything in the clubhouse of a Major League Baseball team.

During pregame availability, I interviewed Lorenzo Cain while he was eating pancakes. I then asked Ned Yost about Cain's season, which was going splendidly to that point. In the fourth inning a few hours later, the game between the Royals and the Tampa Bay Rays was delayed because of rain. Two hours later, the grounds crew pulled up the tarp and began to dry the infield. But before long, the tarp covered the field again, and freezing rain and big, puffy snowflakes fell from the sky.

The Christmas favorite "Let it snow! Let it snow! Let it snow!" delighted fans on the PA system. Later, Royals players emerged from the clubhouse and took pictures of the winter wonderland. Mike Moustakas and Alcides Escobar even went for a slide across the tarp on their bellies. Finally, the game was called just after 4:30 p.m., and a winter weather advisory was in effect.

I remember driving home in the snow thinking how lucky I was that I accomplished a lifelong goal. I got to cover the Royals, and in my mind there was always a better probability of that happening than me playing third base. It snowed a ½ inch that May day. Prior to that, the last time there was measurable snowfall in May in Kansas City was in 1907. What a first day on the job!

In the years since, there have been many memorable moments for the Royals, and for me, that stand out. I hope you enjoy reading about them as well as the ones that came before. I want to thank Sarah Younger for her hard work and believing in this project. I also want to thank the Royals, the Kauffman Foundation, and everyone who contributed to this book and my friends and family for their support. I can't name everyone, but I do want to give a special shout out to Jess Coffey.

"Nothin' stops me in my SUV!"

From playing "Have you met Deters?" to bouncing around story ideas for over a decade, and for this book, your friendship means the world to me. And thank God for your beautiful wife, Michelle, and daughter, Eve, who are Royals fans just like their dad.

The reason I decided to write this book was for the fans. And I hope this book is something you enjoy. While writing it, I also wanted to make it more than a history lesson. I wanted to find new stories and make it more of a celebration book. So now let's celebrate the miracle that is the Kansas City Royals.

PART ONE

START OF SOMETHING SPECIAL

A great business man and humanitarian, Royals founder Ewing Kauffman brought baseball back to Kansas City in 1969. (Courtesy *Ewing Marion Kauffman Foundation*)

1

Birth of a Franchise

Mr. K Steps Up to the Plate

Ewing Kauffman needed a hobby. That's what his wife, Muriel, and his doctor told him. They figured it would help relieve stress and lengthen his life, perhaps another twenty-five years. Kansas City, meanwhile, needed a baseball team. Together, Kauffman and Kansas City made a perfect match.

Following the 1967 season, Charlie Finley moved the A's out west to Oakland, and Kansas City was without a Major League Baseball team for the first time in twelve years. Enter Kauffman, then a fifty-one-year-old who made his coin running Marion Laboratories, a pharmaceutical company that he started in his basement with a $5,000 investment but grew to a billion-dollar company. Kauffman knew how to make money, but he didn't know much about baseball. He just knew Kansas City deserved a team.

In 1955, Kansas City became major league for the first time when Chicago businessman Arnold Johnson, who owned Municipal Stadium in Kansas City, Missouri, paid $3.5 million for the Philadelphia Athletics and moved them to the

Midwest. Until the A's came to town, the Kansas City Blues—the Triple-A affiliate of the New York Yankees—were the primary tenant. Upon arrival, it seemed the A's had a bright future as they had some good ballplayers, but nothing about the A's' tenure in Kansas City was remotely bright. They had a losing season in each of their thirteen years in Kansas City.

There also were some questionable things going on behind the scenes with the club. For starters, Johnson's ownership bid was largely approved thanks to lobbying by the Yankees. Johnson owned Yankee Stadium and Connie Mack Stadium in Philadelphia as well, and to buy the A's, Johnson had to sell his rights to Yankee Stadium to a friend who also was a Chicago businessman. There also were several questionable trades between the A's and Yankees over the years, including the trade following the 1959 season that sent twenty-four-year-old Roger Maris to the Yankees in a package deal for some aging veterans.

Deals like that were just one reason many believed the A's and Yankees were in cahoots in an effort to flatten the Kansas City franchise while the Yankees reaped the rewards and Johnson lined his own pockets. After Johnson's death, Finley became the A's owner in December 1961. By 1962, he already was looking to move the team.

In January 1964, Finley signed an agreement to move the team to Louisville. The team was going to be called the Louisville Athletics until the AL owners rejected the move. A few weeks later, Finley requested to move the team to Oakland, but that request also was denied.

In February 1964, Finley agreed to a new four-year lease to keep the A's in Kansas City, but he was still intent on moving the team as soon as possible. And in September, Finley announced the A's were for sale for $8 million. A local ownership group tried to buy the club for $5 million, but Finley rejected the bid.

Following another last-place finish in 1967, Finley formally requested a move to Oakland. The owners were growing tired of Finley's constant battles with Kansas City, and they dreaded the prospect of litigation. Baseball also was looking to add another team to the sunny California landscape, so the A's move to Oakland was approved on October 18 with the promise that Kansas City, Seattle, Montreal, and San Diego would be awarded expansion franchises by no later than 1971.

Not satisfied, Missouri Senator Stuart Symington threatened to revoke MLB's antitrust exemption if Kansas City wasn't awarded a team earlier. In November 1967, Ernie Mehl, who was sports editor of the *Kansas City Star*, and Earl Smith, an avid supporter of pro ball in Kansas City, asked Kauffman if they could submit his name with the formal franchise application, and Kauffman agreed.

In December 1967, Kauffman and his wife met with California Angels owner Gene Autry and discussed his experiences founding baseball's previous expansion team. After the meeting, Kauffman, with Muriel's insistence, was convinced he should become owner of the Kansas City franchise. In January 1968, four other prospective ownership groups emerged, but only Kauffman's bid was seriously considered by the AL owners. Then, on January 11, 1968, Kauffman was awarded the franchise for $5.3 million.

"Kansas City has been good to me, and I want to show I can return the favor," Kauffman said after being named owner.

In March 1968, Kauffman began a name-the-team contest that was open to the public. The Canaries, Caps, Capsules, Eagles, Kauffs, Kauffies, Kauffers, Kings, Plowboys, Pythons, and Stars were among the names of the 17,000 entries submitted. Kauffman initially had a preference for the Kings, Eagles, and Stars, but the winning entry was Royals, named in honor of the city's American Royal parade, which began in 1899 and today still brings thousands of hogs, cattle, and sheep to the area for the annual livestock show, rodeo, and barbecue contest.

The team colors became blue and white—the same colors as Kauffman's horseracing stable—and artists at Kansas City's Hallmark Cards began designing concepts of the team logo. Some were pretty unique, including a cow that instead of bellowing out, "moo" bellowed, "Kansas City Royals."

Eventually, the Royals chose a gold crown atop a royal-blue shield with the letters K, C, and R inside. Later, after a civic effort to promote Kansas City as a glamorous city and not just another landlocked cow town in the Midwest, references to the team's livestock origins began to fade as quickly as the Royals became baseball's model franchise under Kauffman.

Lucky and the Lady

Julia Irene Kauffman was a teenager when she met Ewing Kauffman, her adopted father, for the first time.

"I liked him immediately," said Julia, who serves as the chairman and chief executive officer of the Muriel McBrien Kauffman Foundation, which supports the performing arts in Kansas City.

However, when her mother, Muriel, met Kauffman for the first time poolside at the Deauville Hotel in Miami in 1961, well, that's another story.

"She was not impressed," Julia said.

Kauffman was in Miami attending a meeting on behalf of Marion Labs. Muriel's mother, Eileen, was on the Toronto Board of Education, and it just so hap-

Ewing and Muriel Kauffman were Royalty in Kansas City. Here they are being honored at old Municipal Stadium. (Courtesy *Ewing Marion Kauffman Foundation*)

pened that there was an education meeting in the Sunshine State, and she asked Muriel to go along.

At the pool, Kauffman, an avid swimmer, was swimming laps and performing rather acrobatic dives and flips, which caught Muriel's attention. When he got out of the pool, Eileen was calling for a drink from the steward, to no avail. Kauffman then walked up, introduced himself, and offered to buy drinks.

Muriel wasn't interested (in Ewing), but Eileen was all for having a drink. So to the hotel bar they all went. Kauffman was smitten by Muriel from the start, and eventually his persistence paid off. When Muriel returned to Toronto, their long-distance courtship began.

The couple wed on February 28, 1962, in Prairie Village, Kansas, a suburb of Kansas City. Together, Ewing and Muriel Kauffman became Kansas City's most vivacious and influential couple. But they were uniquely different, especially in their upbringing.

Kauffman was born September 21, 1916, on a farm in Garden City, Missouri. His father, John, and mother, Effie, moved the family to Creighton, Missouri, not long after Kauffman was born. After the first grade, Kauffman was advanced to the third grade. On Saturday nights, when Kauffman was still just a boy, his parents would invite family and friends over to play pinochle, and young Ewing would watch from his father's side.

While living in Creighton, the family suffered hardship. Ewing's father lost his right eye in an accident while loading cattle, and rain ruined the family's crops three years in a row. When he was eight, the family relocated to Kansas City. Kauffman sold fish and delivered eggs from his aunt's farm to people in the neighborhood, played baseball, and he and his dog, Larry, were inseparable.

At age eleven, Kauffman was diagnosed with endocarditis, an inflammation of the inner lining of the heart that causes leakage of the heart valves. His doctor ordered him to stay in bed for a year, so his mother kept him entertained with books. Kauffman, a speed reader, read forty or fifty books a month. He read biographies on all the presidents and the Bible twice. But his favorite book was *Dr. Hudson's Secret Journal.* The general theme of the book is if you do right to others, good things will come to you, and Kauffman took that to heart.

Kauffman's mother was a school teacher and his father was an outdoorsman. Though they divorced in 1928, both were active participants in Kauffman's childhood. On trips, he and his father would compete to see who could add, subtract, multiply, and divide the numbers on the cars' license plates as they passed by. A Boy Scout and Sea Scout, Kauffman later played football and graduated from Westport High School in 1934.

In the depths of the Great Depression, Kauffman hitchhiked and rode railcars to Colorado to see the Rocky Mountains. He once considered joining the Civilian Conservation Corps—a public work relief program that built roads and dams and promoted environmental conservation as part of President Franklin D. Roosevelt's New Deal—but Kauffman's parents convinced him to return to Kansas City and go to college.

For two years, he attended Junior College of Kansas City and worked part-time at a laundry facility. After graduation in June 1936, Kauffman began working at the laundromat on a full-time basis. In December 1941, Kauffman married

Marguerite Blackshire. In January 1942, just six weeks after the bombing of Pearl Harbor, Kauffman reported to the United States Naval Training Station in Great Lakes, Illinois.

Assigned to the *Lauraleen*—a converted passenger ship that transferred troops, escorted other ships, and guarded against German submarine attacks—Kauffman became a skilled signalman, using flags and flashing lights to communicate with other ships. Below deck in the barracks, Kauffman and other sailors passed the time playing cards.

When it came to gambling, Kauffman rarely lost, and aboard the ship he amassed a small fortune—about $90,000—and earned the nickname "Lucky," which he wasn't too fond of.

"It embarrassed him," Julia said.

One night while aboard the *Lauraleen* off the coast of Cuba, Kauffman believed their convoy of about fifty ships was heading on a dangerous course that would leave them aground. The ships were supposed to make a turn at one in the morning, and Kauffman's sightings that night didn't coincide with those of the navigational officer. Kauffman had the ships eight miles farther ahead than what he did.

Ewing Kauffman, who was always popular with the fans, signs an autograph at Marion Day at a Royals game. (Courtesy *Ewing Marion Kauffman Foundation*)

But the captain naturally sided with the navigational officer over Kauffman, who was just a seaman first class.

Kauffman returned to his bunk that night positive his sights were correct. So he got up and woke the captain.

"I think there's a mistake in our navigation, and we better make our turn earlier," Kauffman said.

"You better be right, Lucky," the captain replied.

Kauffman's calculations were correct. Had they turned thirty minutes later, three of the ships would have hit an island. When Kauffman's ship got to New York, the captain made him an ensign and his new navigational officer. With the end of World War II, Kauffman was released from active military duty on November 16, 1945, and he returned to Kansas City.

One Sunday in 1947, he saw an ad for a pharmaceutical salesman for Lincoln Laboratories and was immediately intrigued. Kauffman knew little about the pharmaceutical business, but what got his attention was that applicants would take an aptitude test.

Kauffman applied, took the test, and got the job. He received no salary, no benefits, and worked on a 20 percent commission. Kauffman, however, with his mild-mannered enthusiasm, was a natural salesman. In his first year, he made more money than the president of the company, so his territory was reduced. In his second year, Kauffman still made an exceptional amount of money, so his territory was cut again.

Not liking the way he was being treated, Kauffman quit. He then dipped into his savings and in June 1950 started Marion Labs with one "associate." Himself. Kauffman didn't like using the word "employee" because he felt it had a bad connotation, so he chose to use "associate." Kauffman also decided to use his middle name for the name of his business so customers wouldn't think it was a one-man operation, and, of course, it worked.

In the first year, the company made just $1,000 profit. But in the years that followed, Marion Labs flourished. In 1970, net sales topped $30 million, and by the time the company merged with Merrell Dow in 1989, Marion was worth about $1 billion.

Tragedy, however, struck the Kauffman family when his company was booming as Marguerite, who had long suffered from health issues, died just before Christmas in 1960. The following year, Kauffman met Muriel McBrien, daughter of Toronto politician Fred McBrien. Muriel was a sports fan growing up. She liked to watch the local baseball team, which was the Maple Leafs at the time. She also got a law degree from Osgoode Hall. She was married to Lorne Dennie until his death a couple of years before she met Kauffman. Ewing and Muriel were literally as different in some aspects as night and day.

Kauffman was early to bed, early to rise. He also slept in four-hour increments, something he did while in the Navy. Muriel, meanwhile, was more outgoing. After Kauffman went to bed, she would often call friends and say, "The old guy's asleep again." Muriel and friends would then go out and party until two in the morning. This group sometimes included Yankees owner George Steinbrenner.

Ironically, according to Julia, Kauffman considered Steinbrenner and Charlie Finley "great friends," though Julia said her father was "a little annoyed" at Finley for moving the A's to Oakland.

As First Lady of the Royals, Muriel was instrumental in many design aspects of the club, and she also was in charge of Kauffman's wardrobe. Muriel often bought him Royal blue suits that he would wear at games.

Ewing and Muriel were always eager to please the home crowd, and during the seventh inning stretch, they would waive to the fans from their suite. A seemingly unlikely pair when they first met, Ewing and Muriel Kauffman were beloved not because of their wealth, but because they were just like the Royals themselves.

"(They were) marvelous," Julia said. "They were a team."

Ewing and Muriel Kauffman were quite visible at the ballpark. Here they are in the Royals dugout before a game in Kansas City. (Courtesy *Ewing Marion Kauffman Foundation*)

Constructing a Team

To build the first team for a franchise that millions would grow to love, Ewing Kauffman, in one of his first moves as owner in January 1968, hired Cedric Tallis as general manager. Tallis was vice president and director of operations for the Angels and helped oversee the construction of Anaheim Stadium, so he was a perfect fit for Kauffman and his new franchise.

Kauffman's baseball knowledge was limited, so he quickly got out of the way. Tallis then began the process of instituting a minor league system and preparing for the upcoming June amateur draft and the expansion draft in October. Tallis also hired veteran scouts, including Art Stewart, who had been a scout with the Yankees for seventeen years, and Charlie Metro, who was a scout with the Reds and became the Royals director of personnel. Tallis also brought in Syd Thrift, Lou Gorman (farm director), John Schuerholz, Jack McKeon, and Herk Robinson, all of whom would go on to become GMs in their careers.

Before the draft, the Royals signed a few experienced players to beef up their eventual MLB squad. But with their first pick in the draft, which came in the fourth round, the Royals selected seventeen-year-old shortstop Kenneth O'Donnell. O'Donnell never made the big leagues, but the Royals picked up some talent. In the 22nd round, they picked Paul Splittorff, a lanky left-hander who went on to pitch fourteen seasons for the Royals and became the team's all-time winningest pitcher with 167 wins.

In August 1968, the Royals were awarded the Omaha minor league franchise, and in September Kauffman created the Royal Lancers, a team of boosters whose job was to sell season tickets. That same month, Tallis hired Joe Gordon as manager.

Gordon had been a standout second baseman with the Yankees and managed the A's in 1961. He lasted just one season with the Royals.

The Royals selected Baltimore pitcher Roger Nelson with their first pick in the expansion draft and Joe Foy with their second pick. The Royals later selected pitcher Al Fitzmorris from the White Sox organization. Fitzmorris, a Western movie buff, knew little about the Royals but had heard of Kansas City.

"I thought it was a cow town," said Fitzmorris, who played for the Royals from 1969 to 1976. "I seriously did."

In all, the Royals drafted thirty players in the expansion draft, and in March 1969, they opened their first spring training in Fort Myers, Florida. A month later, it was time for The Show.

Kansas City Royals broadcaster Denny Matthews speaks after receiving the Ford C. Frick Award during the National Baseball Hall of Fame Induction Ceremony on July 29, 2007, in Cooperstown, N.Y. Matthews has been calling Royals games on the radio since the team's first season in 1969. (Courtesy *Baseball Hall of Fame*)

2

Play Ball!

The Voice of the Royals

The first Royals game was played on April 8, 1969, at Municipal Stadium. The Royals won 4-3 in 12 innings, and the first person to ever say "Royals win!" on the radio was Denny Matthews.

Matthews joined the Royals when he was just twenty-five. Back then, he was teamed with veteran Buddy Blattner, but after Blattner retired in 1975, Matthews took over the primary spot. He was then teamed with Fred White, who was on the Royals broadcast team from 1973 to 1998, and Matthews has been broadcasting with Ryan Lefebvre—who also does TV—since 1999.

Matthews grew up in Bloomington, Illinois, and played baseball and football at Illinois Wesleyan. He was an infielder and had an opportunity to sign with the Giants following his sophomore season but stayed in school. Matthews's big break came when the Royals picked him from more than 300 applicants.

The four expansion teams were starting in 1969, and Matthews didn't have much of a résumé then, so he called the Cardinals and asked them if he could make a game tape. The Cardinals obliged, and Matthews and a friend called the game. He sent the tape to the four expansion teams and hoped for the best.

The Royals whittled it down to three candidates, and Matthews was one of them. They asked him to meet with Blattner in his native St. Louis, so he did. Blattner, who played five seasons in the big leagues and began his broadcasting career in 1950, talked baseball with Matthews for hours at the meeting. A few days later, Matthews got the job.

One of Matthews's favorite subjects to talk about was and still is Ewing Kauffman. On occasion when he wasn't on air, Matthews would slip down to Kauffman's suite.

"The best time was probably the late-'80s into the early-'90s, and sometimes he would be down in his suite all by himself just smoking his pipe and watching the game," Matthews said. "There would be nobody in there, and every once in a while I would wander down there and spend two or three innings and just sit and chat with him, not necessarily about baseball at all. We'd talk about business and life and everything."

Matthews isn't known for being overly enthusiastic on calls, but his trademark phrase "*and gone*" after a home run is part of Royals tradition. In 2007, Matthews, the Ford Frick Award winner, was inducted into baseball's Hall of Fame.

In 2015, Matthews signed a four-year contract to keep calling games for the Royals through the 2018 season. That season, Matthews will become just the third broadcaster in MLB history to reach fifty seasons with the same club, joining Vin Scully, who retired after sixty-seven years with the Brooklyn/Los Angeles Dodgers, and Jaime Jarrín, who in 2016 completed his fifty-eighth year handling the Dodgers' Spanish broadcasts.

Matthews has broadcast Royals games in parts of six different decades, and through it all one thing has always been a constant in his mind. It's what helps keep him coming to the ballpark day after day and year after year.

"Each game is different, so you hope for a good game," Matthews said. "I hope for a good game. I hope for both teams to play well. Then it's a good game, and it's a good broadcast. Sometimes one team is going to play well and the other team not at all. Those games aren't that great, but that's just the way it goes. That's baseball."

His Noble Experiment

Conventional wisdom has it that it takes ten years for an expansion baseball team to become a World Series champion. Ewing Kauffman didn't want to wait that long. So Kauffman began looking for a way to acquire talent other than through the draft.

One day, Kauffman had an idea. It was bold, original, and innovative, like Kauffman himself. Kauffman wondered what if Royals scouts signed raw athletes who were overlooked in the draft and taught how to play baseball? Kauffman believed the idea had potential, and he was right.

In August 1970, Kauffman established the Royals Baseball Academy, an idea many believed was forty years ahead of its time. Kauffman purchased 121 acres of land and built a beautiful complex in Sarasota, Florida, that had a swimming pool, tennis courts, cafeteria, and dormitory. Kauffman's wife, Muriel, even picked the colors of the bed sheets and pillow cases for the rooms.

Syd Thrift became the academy's director, and the Royals held tryouts in fourteen states, evaluating more than 7,600 athletes. One of them was a local kid named Frank White who went on to play for the Royals from 1973 to 1990 and became one of the best second baseman to ever play the game.

White grew up in Kansas City, not far from old Municipal Stadium. He graduated from Lincoln High, but the school didn't have a baseball team, so he played in summer leagues. Just shy of his twentieth birthday, White was already married with a child and working for Metals Protection Plating, a local sheet metal company, making $100 a week when he heard about the Royals tryout that would be held in June 1970. White asked for two days off so he could attend the tryout at the old ballpark, and his boss agreed.

"Baseball was going through a transition when Mr. Kauffman took over the team in '68," White said. "There was a redevelopment of the scouting system and that's why the academy was so prominent because it gave the Royals another opportunity to find players who were looked over in the draft. A lot of scouts didn't go in the inner cities to scout the African American players at that time. So he wanted a different way to find players other than the traditional scouting system and that's where I came into play in terms of being a member of the Royals first Baseball Academy class, so he definitely had some insight there."

White was one of eight players out of 300 who tried out to be selected for the Royals Academy, and he was soon off to Florida. For $48 a month, players would play baseball and get a free education. After 6 a.m. wake-up calls, players would eat breakfast. Breakfast was mandatory, and players were fined $10 if they skipped the meal.

After breakfast, they were bused to Manatee Junior College, where they learned skills like public speaking and money management in the morning

Frank White was the first—and best—graduate of the Royals Baseball Academy. White played for the Royals from 1973 to 1990 and won eight Gold Gloves. He also is considered one of the best second basemen to ever play the game. (Courtesy *Topeka Capital-Journal*)

before concentrating on baseball in the afternoon. Various tests to determine a player's eyesight, speed, coordination, and personality traits were conducted by a staff that included a psychologist who had worked for NASA and the Office of Naval Research. On the field, players received instruction from coaches and baseball greats, including Ted Williams. In August 1971, the Royals sent scout Art Stewart to check on White's progress.

"I went down and evaluated our first class of the Baseball Academy, and Frank was in it," Stewart said. "He was playing shortstop, and you saw the great defensive potential then, and at that age he was just a young kid.

"He was signed out of the tryout camp, and a lot of people in the front office were skeptical of his age. They thought we had somebody who was much older than Frank really was. So they said when you write him up be careful. So it just so happened that while I was down there covering the club, he wanted to buy a car and one of the coaches had to go cosign for him. That's when we found out he really was that young."

In all, the academy produced fourteen big leaguers during its existence, most notably White, Ron Washington, and UL Washington. Ron Washington, like White, was a member of the academy's first class that graduated in December 1971. The first class dominated the competition, going 40-13 and winning the Gulf Coast League title. The team also led the league in batting average, steals, and ERA.

Later, UL Washington, a shortstop, made it to the big leagues with the Royals in 1977. His story of how he got into the academy is quite a tale.

Washington was a high school football player from Oklahoma who hadn't really played much baseball. His brother was working part-time as an usher at Municipal Stadium, and he asked Lou Gorman if his brother could come up for a tryout. Gorman gave the OK, and Washington showed up to the tryout in a sweatshirt. He carried an old glove and had a toothpick in his mouth, a habit that became something of a trademark throughout his career.

Washington first got Gorman's attention with his blazing speed. Then he really got Gorman's attention when he missed every ball that came his way while fielding grounders at shortstop. Finally, a Royals official rolled the ball to Washington so they could see his arm strength. Turns out, Washington's arm was a laser. Then it came time to test his batting prowess. He swung and missed so badly Gorman initially thought Washington might have a vision problem.

Intrigued, Gorman told Thrift that Washington was worth taking a chance on, and he was selected for the academy and would undergo further testing. When the results came back, his scores were off the charts. He failed everything except the vision test.

Many in the organization wanted Washington removed from the program, including Kauffman, who received reports on new players in his academy. One day, Kauffman invited Gorman to have breakfast with him in his office at Marion Labs to discuss the group of new players, but the one Kauffman really wanted to

UL Washington was another graduate of the Royals Baseball Academy. He made it to the big leagues in 1977 and played eight seasons with the Royals. Washington also was pretty good at juggling. (Courtesy *Topeka Capital-Journal*)

talk about was Washington. In his book *High and Inside: My Life in the Front Offices of Baseball*, Gorman recalled the meeting with Kauffman.

"Why is this young man in our program?" Kauffman asked.

"Mr. K, this young man has great speed, great eyesight, and has played very little baseball," Gorman replied. "He is the perfect prototype of what you're trying to prove. If we can make him a ballplayer, we're proving your theory."

Kauffman still wasn't convinced Washington should be in the academy, but he opted to let him stay with one caveat.

"He better be able to play, for your sake!" Kauffman told Gorman.

Washington went on to play for the Royals for eight years, forming a potent double-play duo with White from 1979 to 1983. The academy, however, closed in 1975 as a cost-cutting measure partly due to the delays of constructing a new stadium for the Royals.

Many years after the academy closed, Stewart and Kauffman got together in his office and reminisced about the good old days. But something was on Kauffman's mind. Mr. K usually got everything right, but this time he thought he had done wrong.

"Art, the biggest mistake I made was letting them talk me out of keeping the Baseball Academy. It was the biggest mistake I made," Kauffman told Stewart that day.

Kauffman was once so enthralled with his experiment, he considered concentrating on it full-time. Had he done so, it might still be around.

"That was his crown jewel," Stewart said. "And it was just a shame. Too bad they closed it down. So many innovations from it. So many innovations."

Known for its beautiful fountains and royal crown atop a giant scoreboard, Kauffman Stadium has been home to the Royals since 1973. The ballpark originally opened as Royals Stadium but was renamed in honor of late owner Ewing Kauffman in 1993. "The K" has played host to the 1973 and 2012 All-Star Games. (Courtesy *Jeff Deters*)

Home of the Royals

In June 1967, a $100 million bond issue—including $43 million for football and baseball stadiums—was presented to the voters of Jackson County. Chiefs owner Lamar Hunt and Chiefs chairman of the board Jack Steadman were at the forefront of the push for two new stadiums.

Early on there were discussions about having a multipurpose stadium, but Hunt and Steadman believed it didn't make sense for them to get attached to a baseball team that might not be there because of Charlie Finley. They also believed that if both teams shared a stadium, the city could wind up having a stadium too small for football and too large for baseball.

So when the initiative went to ballot, the vote required a two-thirds majority to pass. Skeptics figured it wouldn't pass. But it did. Then in October, Finley moved

Cy Young Award winner Zack Greinke is captured on the famous crown scoreboard at Kauffman Stadium in September 2009. (Courtesy *Frank Romeo / Shutterstock.com*)

the A's to Oakland, leaving Kansas City with the prospect of having a new stadium but no one to play in it. But those fears were short-lived, as Ewing Kauffman was awarded the team three months later.

The Kansas City architectural firm Kivett and Myers was the lead designer on the two stadiums, and groundbreaking began in July 1968. Part of the original design of the Truman Sports Complex was to have a rolling roof in between the stadiums so games could be played without interruption due to weather. But plans for the rolling roof were scrapped when the project came in over budget as two strikes by construction workers caused delays and drove up costs.

Kauffman and Hunt pumped in millions of their own money to get their stadiums up to snuff, with Kauffman shelling out $2 million for the original twelve-story crown scoreboard in center field and another $750,000 on the stadium's signature fountains, which was the idea of his wife, Muriel.

The plan was to have both stadiums operational for the 1972 seasons, but when it became clear the baseball stadium wouldn't be ready by April, efforts shifted to complete Arrowhead Stadium, which opened on August 12, 1972.

During the winter of 1972–73, Frank White, who was still in the minor leagues, needed some supplemental income to support his family. One day his phone rang. It was Kauffman. His chauffer then took White to the union hall where he got his first union card. White worked on the construction crew at the stadium. Sealing floors and smoothing cement were among his laborious duties.

"There was mixed feelings there because I was still a young player—twenty-two years old," White said. "And the union pay was much better than what I was making as a ballplayer, and I thought about that being a job that I would want to do."

White, however, stuck with baseball, which at the time seemed about as daunting as building a state-of-the-art stadium that would have three tiers and 40,793 seats.

"There were a lot of days during the winter where you look down on the field and wonder if you are ever going to be able to take that on and become a major league player," White said.

The first game played at Royals Stadium—the stadium's original name before it was changed to Kauffman Stadium in 1993—was on April 10, 1973. The Royals played the Rangers and won 12-1. Paul Splittorff got the victory.

First baseman John Mayberry slugged the first home run in stadium history in the fifth inning and had four RBIs. White, meanwhile, got his first call-up to the big leagues on June 12, 1973.

"Then I realized that I was setting my feet on the field at then-Royals Stadium for the first time," White said.

White's arrival came one month before Kansas City hosted the 1973 All-Star Game. Mayberry, center fielder Amos Otis, who was the team's first five-tool player, and second baseman Cookie Rojas represented the Royals. Otis had two hits and an RBI and Mayberry had a hit, but the AL lost 7-1.

In 2009, a $250 million stadium renovation was completed, giving the ballpark a new scoreboard, more concessions, and wider concourses, among other amenities. The All-Star Game returned in July 2012, and designated hitter Billy Butler represented the Royals. Butler went 0-for-2, and the AL lost 8-0.

Today, in the age of corporations purchasing naming rights, Kauffman Stadium is the only ballpark in the AL that is named after a person, and the venue is sixth oldest in baseball. But it remains one of the most beautiful stadiums in all of sports, and it's hard to imagine the Royals playing anywhere else.

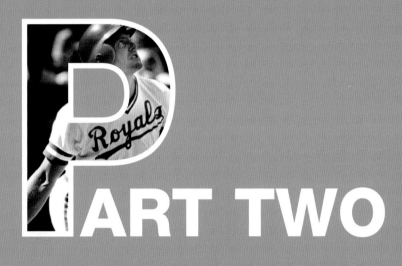

PART TWO

RISING TO THE TOP

Steve Busby became the first pitcher in history to throw no-hitters in each of his first two seasons in the big leagues. (Courtesy *Topeka Capital-Journal*)

3

Setting the Standard

The No-Hit Kid

It has been more than ninety years since Lou Gehrig replaced Wally Pipp at first base for the Yankees. But in the Kansas City locker room during the 1970s, everyone, including right-handed pitcher Steve Busby, was still talking about how Pipp once took the day off because of a headache and the then-backup Gehrig took his job for good.

"Wally Pipp was a very popular name back then," Busby said. "That was on everybody's mind. If you don't come out of the lineup, nobody has a chance to take your spot."

This is really the tell-all of Busby's career as a Royal. In 1973, the Royals had reason to believe their immediate future was bright, and those hopes were in fact realized thanks in part to Busby, their ace. Busby primarily threw just two pitches: a fastball and slider. His stuff was overpowering, and he became the first player in MLB history to throw no-hitters in each of his first two seasons (1973 and 1974).

But in Busby's day the team trainer was not well liked, pitch counts weren't kept track of that well, and injured players were considered unreliable and expendable, and Busby didn't want to be one of those. So he pitched through the pain until he no longer could.

A torn rotator cuff forced him into early retirement after just eight years, ending a brief but brilliant career. Busby was a starter for essentially just three seasons from 1973 to 1975 and won 56 games in that stretch to go with the two no-hitters. The first no-hitter came on April, 27, 1973, and Busby remembers the 3-0 Royals' victory well.

"Cold night in Detroit with the wind blowing off the lake," Busby said. "The Tigers were an older team, and they didn't really feel like hitting too much against a young kid that had no clue where the ball was going. I was pretty wild. I wish I could say effectively wild, but it wasn't. I was wilder than that."

Busby issued six walks that night.

"It was probably a surprise to them every time I threw a strike," Busby said.

Busby's first no-hitter came in just the tenth start of his career. His second no-hitter came on June 19, 1974, at County Stadium in Milwaukee. The Royals won 2-0.

"I had a much better idea of what's going on than the first time," Busby said. "I was kind of in shock the first time, but the second time I had been there and been through that a little bit, especially late in the ballgame. I wasn't nearly as wild. I only walked one. There were a lot of great plays made behind me.

"Cookie Rojas, Amos Otis, and Al Cowens were running all over the outfield tracking down balls. It was a totally different game. It had the same outcome but it was a totally different game."

When Busby played, teams used four-man rotations, and he threw a combined 791 innings and had 45 complete games from 1973 to 1975. Busby was an All-Star in 1974 and 1975, but after the All-Star break in '75, he began to feel pain in his right shoulder. At the time he wasn't sure what it was, but thirteen starts into the 1976 season, Busby was diagnosed with a torn rotator cuff, altering the trajectory of what could have been a stellar career. The rest of the '70s included a series of surgeries, comeback attempts, and questions of what might have been.

"Were there more injuries back then? No, there weren't," Busby said. "You look at it right now and there are more injuries now than there ever has been. Part of that is being able to diagnose problems earlier now. Part of that is having agents who are very concerned about their clients' well-being for the money aspect.

"You tend to have encouragement every time there's a little ache or pain to go get it checked out and get a second opinion and that wasn't the case when we were playing."

Busby missed all of the 1977 season recovering from surgery and appeared in just 40 games over the next three seasons, making his final appearance in August 1980, ending his career having never played in the postseason.

"It was very tough," Busby said. "That's what you play the game for. That's why you play is to get to the highest level you possibly can and to win everything, so that was very tough. I don't feel like my career was complete and never will be.

"I'm not going to say I let everybody down because it wasn't something I could have done anything differently about. But I think I would have loved to have an opportunity to find out if I could have made a difference."

The White Rat

There's an old adage in baseball. Well, it's really more of a question. How much difference can a manger really make? The popular answer is not much, citing the belief that a team that wins ninety games or loses ninety games would not have fared much differently with a different manager.

But there are a few managers who make a difference, repeatedly outwitting their counterpart, and inspiring their players to do great things. Dorrel Norman Elvert "Whitey" Herzog was one of those managers.

Herzog became manager of the Royals on July 25, 1975. He replaced Jack McKeon, who had been fired after a 50-46 start to the season. Herzog was a third-base coach for the California Angels at the time and was living in Independence, Missouri. Herzog had settled there after an eight-year career in the big leagues, including three with the Kansas City A's (1958 to 1960).

Herzog had been a manager before he joined the Royals. Taking over for Ted Williams, Herzog went 47-91 in 1973 with Texas before being fired in his first season. He also went 2-2 with the Angels in 1974 filling in during a coaching change.

With Herzog in the dugout, a new era of Royals baseball began, and "Whiteyball" quickly became synonymous with club. In the AL, power and might have long been the standard recipe for success. But Herzog had a different formula.

Herzog's teams emphasized pitching, speed, and defense instead of home runs. His teams also came up clutch in the late innings. Herzog also placed value on stats such as OBP long before it became a main part of a player's evaluation.

In 1975, the Royals were still in their infancy, but they had already produced two winning seasons and were primed for a third. But they were underachieving, and general manager Joe Burke had his eye on Herzog, whom he had worked with in Texas.

"He said he wanted me to come to Kansas City and be the manager," Herzog said. "I couldn't have stepped into a better situation after having a bad situation in Texas. Joe was there, and the fact that he was wanting me in Kansas City, and (Ewing) Kauffman was wanting me in Kansas City."

The Royals went 41-25 after Herzog took over, finishing the season with a 91-71 record and second place in the division to the A's. On the mound, Steve Busby won 18 games, Al Fitzmorris won 16, and Dennis Leonard won 15. Amos Otis stole 39 bases

As manager of the Kansas City Royals, Whitey Herzog went against the grain in the American League, winning games not by the home run, but by pitching, speed, and defense. Here he is during a game in 1975, his first season with the club. (Courtesy *Baseball Hall of Fame*)

while shortstop Freddie Patek swiped 34 bags and contributed with the glove.

The team's Opening Day second baseman was Cookie Rojas, who had made four straight All-Star Games with the Royals. But Frank White, who began the season on the bench, started to emerge as an everyday player.

"When I put Frank out there, Cookie was a favorite in Kansas City, and the fans loved him," Herzog said. "But Frank, his range and his athletic ability, I'm talking about throwing right, throwing left, coming in on slow-hit balls, going back for popups, he was a complete package."

In 1975, John Mayberry hit 34 homers, Hal McRae was still in his prime, and a young twenty-two-year-old third baseman named George Brett played his position with a reckless abandon and led the league in hits (195) and triples (13). The Royals drafted Brett in the second round of the 1971 draft out of El Segundo

High School in California, and when he was in playing in the minors in Billings, Montana, Art Stewart traveled north for a look at the future Hall of Famer and Kansas City icon.

"The first year, he was invited to the instructional league, and you could see it," Stewart said. "You didn't know he was going to be that great, but you could see the tools. He was a plus runner and had a good arm and swung the bat, but never visualizing what he did.

"But what he did show me was the greatest work ethic I ever saw in a kid. George, you'd come down there and you never saw anybody work harder. And George carried that through his whole career."

As Brett's career took flight, he and Herzog developed quite a friendship. They'd go hunting together, play cards before games, and Brett often was a dinner guest at Herzog's house.

Overtaking the A's

In the summer of 1976, the Royals seemed primed to take the next step. But standing in their way was a familiar giant. The A's had been the dominant team in the division in the 1970s, winning five straight division titles from 1971 to 1975 and three straight World Series titles from 1972 to 1974.

In late September, the Royals and A's met in Oakland. It was the final game of the series, and the Royals' lead in the division had shrunk to 2 ½ games after dropping the first two of the series. A week earlier, Amos Otis was hit in the head by a pitch, and he didn't play much that week. He also missed the first two games of the Oakland series.

"I couldn't get a helmet on," Otis recalled. "I had a knot on my head, and Whitey thought I was gun-shy."

After some prodding from his players, Herzog put Otis back in the lineup for the series finale. The move paid off, as the Royals won 4-0 on the strength of Otis's bat and Larry Gura's arm. Otis went 2-for-4 with a homer, a double, and two RBIs, while Gura threw a complete game. With the win, the Royals also clinched at least a share of the division title. As Otis was getting ready to get on the team bus, he heard a familiar sound.

"I was used to people at the ballpark saying, 'AO! AO!'" Otis said. "I got on the bus, and the whole team was saying it. That's the greatest thing that can happen to you is your teammates acknowledging what you did. That was probably my greatest memory in baseball."

That Royals' win was their 90th of the season. They didn't win again in the regular season, but they didn't need to in order to clinch the division outright. Entering the final three games of the regular season, the Royals' magic number was one, and either a win or an Oakland loss would wrap up the division. On October 1, the Royals were playing the Twins at home in the first game of the series. The Royals lost 4-3, but players and fans stuck around after the game.

On the West Coast, the Angels and A's were in a scoreless tie and headed to extra innings. The Angels ultimately won in 12 innings, and the Royals were division champs and would play in the postseason for the first time.

"Some say we backed into the playoffs that year," Otis said. "I don't see it that way. Once you catch somebody—that was special because we finally beat them."

The Royals got off to a slow start that season, going 5-7. But they led the division by 10 ½ games by mid-July and never relinquished their grip on first place in the standings.

The Royals hit just 65 homers that season, and only two players hit more than 10. Otis hit 18 homers and first baseman John Mayberry hit 13. But the Royals were fast. Seven players stole at least 20 bases, led by shortstop Freddie Patek's 51. Even Hal McRae stole 22 bases, one more than George Brett, who made the All-Star Game for the first time.

Brett Takes the Title

Imagine this: George Brett circling the bases for a home run. That happened 317 times in Brett's career, but in his final at-bat of the 1976 regular season, a lot was on the line. The at-bat ended with Brett running full speed around the bases at Royals Stadium for an inside-the-park home run, giving him a .333 average and his first batting title at age twenty-three.

"It was just one of those things where I stayed healthy and played a lot of games," Brett said. "I stayed consistent and was learning how to play in the major leagues. I was learning how to hit, and I was doing what my hitting coach Charlie Lau told me to do.

"I stuck with the program and I found myself going into the last game of the year in a four-way race: me, Hal McRae, Lyman Bostock, and Rod Carew. I ended up getting three hits to win, so it was a big thrill."

Sounds sort of like a fairy tale, right? A beloved player hitting a home run in his final at-bat in front of the hometown crowd to win a batting title. But that alone wasn't the story.

Kansas City icon George Brett was the face of the Royals franchise from 1973 to 1993. In that time, he won three batting titles, his first in 1976. (Courtesy *Baseball Hall of Fame*)

Brett, McRae, Bostock, and Carew were 1-2-3-4 going into the final three-game series. Bostock and Carew were playing for the Twins, and the Twins were playing the Royals. So someone at Royals Stadium would be crowned batting champ by series' end.

When the final day of the regular season began, Brett, McRae, and Carew were within a percentage point of one another. McRae led the pack, hitting .33078. Brett was second at .33073, and Carew was third at .32945. Bostock was out of the running when he injured his thumb in the series opener and missed the last two games, finishing the year with a .323 average. Carew went 2-for-4, finishing the year at .331.

Brett and McRae started the day by getting two hits in their first three at-bats. Brett was hitting third in the lineup and McRae fourth. McRae led Brett .3326 to .3322 entering the ninth inning. With one out, Brett hit a fly ball to left field.

Steve Brye, who normally played center, probably should have caught the ball easily. Instead, the ball dropped in front of him and bounced over his head. Brye was playing deep, and during his path to the ball, he actually stopped for a moment. After the game, Brett said he thought Brye let it drop.

From the on-deck circle, McRae watched as Brett ran the bases. He then greeted Brett with a high-five after Brett crossed home plate, cutting the deficit to 5-3. McRae could still win the batting title with one more hit. Instead, he grounded out to short, finishing with a .332 average, which gave the batting title to Brett.

McRae was happy for his teammate. But after he grounded out, something bothered him. Citing racism, McRae believed manager Gene Mauch and the Twins had conspired against him so Brett could win the title. McRae tipped his cap to the cheering fans as he left the field. He then turned to the Twins dugout, shouted, and raised his middle finger. An incensed Mauch charged the field, and both benches cleared.

"People don't know the truth," McRae said after the game. "And when I say it, they just think I'm making excuses, when everybody with good vision knows I'm not."

"This is America, and not that much has changed," McRae added. "Too bad in 1976 things are still like that."

Brye insisted he didn't intentionally let the ball drop. Mauch, meanwhile, was appalled by the whole ordeal and visibly shaken after the game. Royals manager Whitey Herzog found himself in a somewhat precarious spot, starting the day before when he held Brett and McRae out of the lineup.

"I told Brett and McRae they weren't going to play Saturday," Herzog said. "But because they were that close to the batting title, and the playoff started on Tuesday, I had them play nine innings on Sunday not to show favoritism to either one."

In the days that followed, Brett offered to share the title with McRae, but that didn't happen. An investigation by AL President Lee MacPhail took place, and no evidence of wrongdoing was found. But that wasn't the end of it. Questions about the incident followed the Royals in the playoffs. And why wouldn't it? They were about to play the Yankees.

4

A Rivalry Begins

Beaten in the Bronx

Baseball is a game of inches. Sometimes the ball lands nestled in a glove for an out, and sometimes it scrapes over the wall and ends a season.

This is what happened to the Royals in Game Five of the 1976 ALCS against the Yankees. With a 6-6 score in the bottom of the ninth, the Yankees' Chris Chambliss turned on closer Mark Littell's first pitch, a towering blast that went high into the night sky at Yankee Stadium and ended up being one of the most memorable walk-off homers in MLB history.

Hal McRae, the Royals' usual designated hitter, was playing right field. He had played there the previous four games because Amos Otis injured his ankle in Game One and didn't play the rest of the series. Al Cowens, the usual starting right fielder, shifted to center, with the 5-foot-11 McRae in right.

As the ball zoomed toward the outfield wall, McRae backed up, turned, and jumped. The ball landed just past his outstretched glove, and the Yankees won 7-6.

"If Cowens would have been playing right field, and Otis center field, Cowens would have caught that ball because he was six inches taller than McRae," Royals manager Whitey Herzog said. "It was just one of those things. It was a geography home run. It wouldn't have been a home run anywhere else."

Before Littell's first pitch, however, there was a lengthy delay. Yankees fans were making their presence felt, throwing batteries and bottles and other things onto the field. When the game finally resumed, Chambliss hit a high fastball that rocketed off his bat.

After the ball landed for a home run, Yankees fans jumped from their seats and ran onto the field to celebrate. The crowd was so massive that Chambliss had to plow through fans as he ran the bases. When Chambliss went to touch third base, the bag was already gone. With the crowd nearly engulfing the entire infield, Chambliss had little choice but to head for the clubhouse.

In the locker room, teammates told Chambliss to run back out and touch home plate. With police escorting him back on the field, Chambliss touched somewhere in the vicinity of where home plate used to be, as it was gone, as well.

An inning earlier, three Royal feet had touched home, tying the score at 6-6 when George Brett blasted a three-run homer deep into the seats in right field to give the Royals a chance. The Royals actually led 2-0 after the first inning as Brett and John Mayberry hit back-to-back homers. But the Royals had problems in the first: starter Dennis Leonard didn't record an out and was pulled after the first four Yankees reached base and two runs had scored.

Paul Splittorff stabilized things, pitching 3 ⅔ innings. His only blemish came when he gave up two runs in the third, which gave the Yankees a 4-3 lead. The Yankees added two more in the sixth before Brett's homer tied it. Had the Yankees not scored in the ninth, the Royals would have had Brett, Mayberry, and McRae due up in the tenth.

The five-game series began with the first two at Royals Stadium. In Game One, the Yankees won 4-1, as Catfish Hunter pitched a complete game. The Royals evened the series with a 7-3 win in Game Two, with Splittorff again coming on in relief of Leonard and rescuing the Royals, throwing 5 ⅔ scoreless.

The Royals lost 5-3 in Game Three, with the Yankees scoring five unanswered to negate a three-run Royal first. The Royals then avoided elimination with a 7-4 victory in Game Four, setting the stage for Game Five.

"We had been in a pennant race with Oakland basically for three years and that gave us some experience playing meaningful games," said catcher Buck Martinez, who played for the Royals from 1969 to 1977. "But in '76 we were a little overwhelmed by the atmosphere of going to Yankee Stadium. We were the upstart Royals, and they were the Yankees."

Though the end result wasn't what the Royals had hoped for, one of the most heated rivalries in sports had been born—a rivalry between a big-market franchise with a storied history of winning World Series and a small-market club that was still in its infancy but rapidly getting better.

"For a team that had only been in existence from 1969 to 1976 and being in the playoffs and being one pitch away or one run away from the World Series, that's a pretty good feat," Brett said.

Best Team Comes Up Short

The Royals have had plenty of good teams over the years, but talk to those in the organization, and they'll tell you that to this day, the 1977 team was a cut above the rest.

That year, the Royals won a franchise-record 102 games and had the best record in baseball. To put it mildly, the Royals were loaded with talent. Armed with 20-game winner Dennis Leonard, 18-game winner Jim Colborn, who also threw a no-hitter that year, and 16-game winner Paul Splittorff, the Royals pitching staff had the best ERA in baseball (3.52), most saves (42), and gave up the fewest hits, runs, and home runs.

The lineup featured George Brett, Frank White, Hal McRae, John Mayberry, Al Cowens, and new catcher Darrell Porter. The Royals also led the league in doubles and triples, and Brett, McRae, Mayberry, and Cowens all hit at least 20 homers. It seemed the Royals were destined to win the pennant.

"It's the best team I ever played on," said center fielder Amos Otis, who hit 17 homers and stole 23 bases that year. "We should have won the World Series."

But the Royals didn't. They were again knocked out of the playoffs with a 5-3 loss to the Yankees in Game Five of the ALCS at Royals Stadium.

"We had the best team," Whitey Herzog said. "We won 102 games. I thought for sure we had the Yankees down at one time. But they got two or three bloop hits in the ninth inning. It was just one of those things."

The Royals led 3-1 after seven innings before the Yankees won it with four unanswered runs, scoring one in the eighth and three more in the ninth. To start the ninth, Herzog went with Leonard, who was pitching on two days' rest after throwing a complete game in the Royals' 6-2 win in Game Three. It also was just the second time all year Leonard had pitched out of the bullpen. It didn't go well.

Leonard gave up a single and a walk, and Herzog handed the ball to left-hander Larry Gura to face the left-handed-hitting Mickey Rivers. Rivers singled, and the Yankees were within a run.

Mark Littell was summoned from the Royals bullpen and got a fly ball to center field, but it was deep enough to score a run, and the game was tied. The Yankees then scored two more on a groundout and a throwing error by Brett for the final margin.

The game still had drama, especially early. In the first inning with McRae aboard, Brett hit a liner that got past Rivers in center. Brett then used a pop-up slide at third. On the way up, Brett gave Yankees third baseman Graig Nettles a little elbow, trying to knock the ball out of his glove. Brett's momentum made him fall forward to his knees, and Nettles kicked Brett in the face.

The bad blood between the two teams had finally spilled over. It started with the way the ALCS ended the year before, and it was evident again in Game Two of the 1977 ALCS, as the Yankees were furious after two hard slides by McRae.

The first incident came in the first inning, when McRae knocked the ball out of shortstop Bucky Dent's glove on a steal attempt. Later in the sixth inning, with Brett at the plate, McRae sent second baseman Willie Randolph flying with a rolling block as he crashed into Randolph, using his hips to break up a double play.

"Brett and McRae could take out the shortstop and second baseman better than anybody I've ever seen play," Herzog said.

With Randolph on the dirt and the ball on the ground, Freddie Patek scored from second, tying the game at 2-2. Now the Yankees were really hot. Manager Billy Martin came out to argue but didn't like what the umpire had to say. Randolph also argued, but he ended up throwing the ball into the Royals dugout in frustration.

In an attempt to stop slides like McRae's, baseball soon implemented the Hal McRae rule, which basically stated that base runners at least had to attempt to touch the base on a slide. But in the interim, many players still went in with the intent to take someone out.

In the bottom of the sixth inning in Game Two, Yankees catcher Thurman Munson went in high to third base with Brett at the bag, causing another somewhat unpleasant scene. So in the first inning of Game Five, after getting kicked in the face, Brett came up swinging and punched Nettles in the head, knocking his hat off.

After Brett's punch, the benches cleared, but no one was thrown out of the game, which ended with Patek grounding into a double play. The outcome might have been different had the series been seven games like it is today, Herzog believes.

"I always wished it would have been a seven-game series," Herzog said." But that's the way it worked. You play all year and the division winners would play five games."

The outcome also might have been different had one notable Royal been in the lineup for Game Five. Mayberry didn't play, as he was benched by Herzog for his poor performance in Game Four.

Mayberry, who usually was one of the first players to the ballpark each day, showed up just a few minutes before the first pitch. It was a day game following a night game, and Mayberry was in no condition to play after a late-night outing.

In four innings in Game Four, Mayberry struck out twice and committed two errors, dropping a foul ball and a routine throw. Herzog then inserted John Wathan at first. After the Game Four loss, Herzog told the media that he pulled Mayberry because his first baseman had a toothache. But everyone knew better.

In the offseason, Littell and Martinez were traded to St. Louis, and Herzog went to management and gave an ultimatum that it was either him or Mayberry. A few days before the start of the 1978 season, Mayberry was sold to Toronto.

Third Time Is Not the Charm

Hitting a home run is a thrill only a select few get to experience in the majors. And even fewer get to know what it's like to hit a home run at Yankee Stadium. George Brett did this three times in Game Three of the 1978 ALCS against New York starter Catfish Hunter, but the Royals still the lost the game and the series in four games, finishing their season for the third straight year with a loss to New York in the playoffs.

"Unfortunately we couldn't get by the Yankees," Brett said.

Brett homered his first three at-bats in Game Three, hitting the first one into the upper deck in right field in the first inning, the second to center field in the third, and the third to right in the fifth. His first two home runs gave the Royals the lead, and his third homer tied it.

The Yankees, however, retook the lead in the sixth, and after the Royals scored two in the eighth off closer Goose Gossage to regain the lead, the Yankees scored two in their half of the inning to win 6-5.

The following night, the Royals lost 2-1 as the Yankees scored two runs on solo homers against Dennis Leonard to win their third straight pennant. The Royals, meanwhile, felt snakebitten.

"They were always the Achilles' heel, so to speak," Leonard said of the Yankees.

The Royals didn't have the best record in baseball that season. The Yankees did with a 100-62 record, eight wins better than the Royals. But in Whitey Herzog's mind the Royals were still the best team.

"We should have won the playoffs," Herzog said.

Brett hit .389 in the ALCS, going 7-for-18 with a double, a triple, and those three homers at Yankee Stadium.

"I didn't try to be a player I wasn't," Brett said. "You get a lot of guys that are not home-run hitters who are trying to hit home runs in key situations. I never tried to hit home runs. I just tried to hit the ball hard somewhere and take my chances."

"When you talk about George Brett, you're talking about something special," Herzog said. "He didn't need a manager. This guy was some ballplayer. He would be out at the ballpark early if he got a bruise, or the night before, he would be in the whirlpool treating himself."

Brett's season began with a trip to the disabled list in late April when he injured his left shoulder breaking up a double play at second base. Brett returned after missing about three weeks and still made the All-Star Game. He was one of four Royals to do so; Frank White, Freddie Patek, and Darrel Porter were the others.

Still, Brett was really the only household name the Royals had when October rolled around and they played the Yankees.

"We always felt like we were as good as the Yankees," White said. "They had the names. They had the big names. And everybody when it came to our team, the only name that the national media seemed to know was George Brett even though we had some very good players on our ballclub."

One of those was Leonard, who won 21 games that season but went 0-2 in the ALCS. Leonard, who grew up in New York and was a Yankees fan as a kid, soon learned to dislike them.

"After 1976, 1977, and 1978, I learned to hate them bad," Leonard said. "To this day I'm not real fond of them."

In 1979, the Royals went 85-77 but missed the playoffs, and Herzog was not retained as manager. Disagreements with Ewing Kauffman and the front office also played a role in his demise. Herzog was replaced with Jim Frey.

5

Good, But Not Good Enough

The Chase for .400

One of the hottest summers on record in Kansas City was in 1980. Hotter yet was George Brett, who sizzled from late May on. His hot streak is one that to this day defies logic and the odds. For a four-month period, no one could get Brett out.

In his career, Brett, who never wore batting gloves, had long been a slow starter the first month of the season, as the cold Kansas City Aprils chilled his hands and his bat. After going hitless in six tries against the A's on May 21, Brett's average was a paltry .247. But entering the season, Brett was a .310 career hitter. So that .247 average was bound to go up once the temperatures began to rise. And Brett heated up nicely, taking America on a ride the game hasn't seen since and might never see again.

"I always liked playing in the heat," Brett said. "I grew up in Southern California and didn't like playing in cold weather. I think that's why my April stats were so bad, but it seemed around the middle of May, around my birthday, it seemed like I'd start swinging the bat a lot better."

In 1980, Kansas City Royals third baseman George Brett took the nation on quite a run as he was trying to become the first player since Ted Williams to hit .400. (Courtesy *Topeka Capital-Journal*)

In that scorcher of a summer, Brett was trying to become the first player to hit .400 since Ted Williams hit .406 in 1941 with the Red Sox. After a hot stretch to close out the month (17-for-40), Brett finished hitting .329 in May. He followed that up by batting .472 in June, .494 in July, and .430 in August.

Baseball has a way of bringing people together. With a 162-game season, that's sort of in its nature. But Brett, the blond-haired boy who was born in West Virginia, raised in California, and became a superstar for the Royals in the Midwest, seemed to do that single-handedly that summer.

Perhaps more than any other sport, baseball is a game of numbers. And .400 is something so dear to the baseball world.

"Believe me, I never thought I was going to hit .400 going into the 1980 season. The highest I had hit was .333 (in 1976) and .329 (in 1979), and for me to be in that uncharted territory . . ." Brett said before pausing. "At first, with six weeks to go, when I went over it, everyone said you got a chance to hit .400, and I started laughing.

"I said, 'Geez, I've never hit higher than .333. I'm seeing the ball good right now, and as a result you're going to get hits.' And when they started talking about .400, I didn't know all of the history of .400 then. And I started hearing more and more about it with Ted Williams in 1941, and all this stuff, and to my amazement I was still over .400 with two weeks to go in the season."

When Williams accomplished the feat in 1941, it came with little fanfare. Back then, hitting .400 wasn't really that big of a deal. When Williams did it that season, it was the twenty-eighth time in MLB history someone hit .400. Ty Cobb and Rogers Hornsby each hit .400 or better three times prior to Williams. But in the thirty-nine years leading up to Brett's run, no one had come close. So by the time Brett was making his charge at the record books, Williams's accomplishment had grown from ordinary to extraordinary, kind of like Brett himself.

On August 17, Brett hit a double to left field in his final at-bat, and the scoreboard at Royals Stadium flashed that Brett was hitting .401. Brett raised his arms, and the crowd of 30,693 cheered.

"Baseball was fun," Brett said. "It was easy, and I just felt like I was going to get a hit every time I walked up to the plate."

Brett's bid for .400 was inescapable. Even Ronald Reagan and Jimmy Carter mentioned Brett as they crisscrossed the country during the 1980 presidential campaign. There were even "George Brett for President" signs at rallies.

"It's just one of those things," Brett said. "You get on a pretty good roll and everybody's going to take advantage of it. If you handle the situation right you can have fun with it. I had fun with it."

But all fun and games aside, everyone wanted Brett to hit .400, including Williams, who was long since retired. Brett's batting average peaked at .407 on August 26 after he went 5-for-5 at Milwaukee.

At one point in the season, the Elias Sports Bureau figured Brett, who was already a perennial All-Star and owner of one batting title, had a 1.9 quadrillion-to-one shot at hitting .400. In early September, however, oddsmakers in Las Vegas gave Brett a 4-to-1 chance to do what was once deemed impossible.

Brett had already done the impossible many times before in his career, and he figured he could do this, as well. At age twenty-seven, Brett also was in the prime of his career. As he closed in on history, newspapers around the country began running the "Brett Watch," a daily update of his performance at the plate. As his pursuit of .400 continued, more national media were sent to wherever Brett was playing that night.

There were so many reporters in the Royals clubhouse that at first the organization wasn't sure what to do. Eventually, the Royals decided Brett would hold a news conference before and after each game. This also came with a cost. Unfortunately for Brett, it made him somewhat isolated from his teammates.

Sometimes after a game, he would miss the team bus back to the hotel as he answered questions from reporters. Finally, when all the questions were asked and answered, Brett and a member of the Royals media relations department would then go to the team hotel.

Brett usually was a media darling. He often joked around with them while flashing that smile of his. He liked the attention. Still does. But eventually the constant questions began to take its toll on Brett, who once snapped at reporters, which was very unlike him. The New York Daily News even ran a headline that said, "Pressure Getting to Brett."

Still, Brett kept hitting. On September 17, Brett returned to the lineup after missing nine games with a wrist injury. The Royals wrapped up the division title that day with a doubleheader split against the Angels, but Brett didn't play in the opener, which was a Royals win. He came on in the nightcap and got two hits, upping his average to .396.

"Back then they didn't have rehab assignments," Brett said. "You just took some BP for a few days and then you were ready to play, and I picked up right where I left off. I was just able to stay within myself and try to do what I was capable of doing."

After getting two hits against the A's on September 19, Brett's batting average was at .400 with 14 games to go in the regular season.

"Then I went out and tried to hit .400 rather than just go out there and have fun, see the ball, hit the ball," Brett said. "I started pressing a little bit when the average fell below .400."

A six-game road trip to Seattle and Minnesota was next, and by the end of the fifth game, which was the second game of the three-game series against the Twins, Brett's average had dipped to .384. By this time, most of the media that was covering Brett had already left, convinced he couldn't do it.

Not so fast.

The next day, Brett was held out of the starting lineup but later came on as a pinch-hitter and hit a grand slam in the sixth inning, but the Royals lost 8-7, their eighth consecutive defeat. Brett hated losing. It irked him. The same was true for the Royals. So they won five of six to close out the regular season and finished with a record of 95-67. But they also wanted .400.

The Royals finished the regular season with a six-game homestand, three each against Seattle and Minnesota. In the Seattle series, Brett caught fire. In the opener, he went 3-for-6 and hit the game-winning home run. The next game, he went 3-for-3 with a home run, pushing his average to .391 with four games remaining.

The Royals crunched numbers and figured Brett needed 10 hits in those four games to reach .400. Difficult, yes, but certainly not impossible for Brett.

"It's not over," Brett told himself.

But it was.

Brett went 0-for-2 in the series finale against the Mariners and went a combined 3-for-7 in the first two games against the Twins. Brett sat out the regular-season finale, resting up for the Yankees, who once again waited in the playoffs. Brett finished the regular season with a .390 average.

Since Brett's historic run, a few players have made a run at .400. All have failed. The closest statistically was Tony Gwynn, who was hitting .394 when the players' strike canceled the season on August 12, 1994. But it's worth remembering that Brett was hitting .400 with a couple weeks to go in the season, making his the most serious threat to the magic number since Williams.

In today's 24/7 media cycle, and with teams having stacked bullpens, Brett said he doesn't believe anyone will ever hit .400 again. That may well be true, because if you really think about it, if Brett couldn't do it, who could?

"I think the game is tougher now," Brett said. "Ted Williams, as good a hitter as he was, and the guys that hit .400, they could probably hit .400 (today). But I don't see anybody in Major League Baseball right now doing that."

Though he didn't hit .400, 1980 was still a wonderful season for Brett. He was named AL MVP despite missing 45 games with various injuries. As great as Brett's run at .400 was, here's something really astounding. In the 117 games Brett played, he had 118 RBIs, becoming the first player since Williams's former teammate Walt Dropo in 1950 to average more than an RBI per game.

Maybe even more astonishing, Brett had more home runs (24) that season than strikeouts (22). How's that for one hot summer?

"I had a good run," Brett said. "I thought I might have another run at it, but I just never got that hot again."

Dethroning the Yankees

With one mighty swing, George Brett changed history. On October 10, 1980, Brett, the Royals' left-handed-hitting superstar, stood at the plate facing Yankees closer Goose Gossage in the top of the seventh inning in Game Three of the ALCS at Yankee Stadium. In their past postseason meetings, the Yankees had the advantage when it came to late-inning relief because they used top-notch relievers, while the Royals sometimes used starters to try to finish games.

That didn't go so well for the Royals, who were trailing 2–1 on the scoreboard with two outs when Brett came up to bat at that crucial moment in Game Three. In some ways, the Royals' fate in the series hinged on Brett's at-bat. The Royals led the series 2–0, but a Yankee comeback wasn't out of the question, and an out by Brett could have turned the series in the Yankees' favor.

A home run by Brett, however, would likely put the Royals in the World Series for the first time in franchise history. So there stood Brett at the plate with two on after Willie Wilson doubled off Yankees starter Tommy John and UL Washington hit an infield single against Gossage. Brett was 0-for-2 on the night and just 2-for-10 in the series, getting both hits in Game One. On Gossage's first pitch, Brett drilled a fastball into the upper deck in right field for a three-run home run. Brett took his time rounding the bases, enjoying the moment.

His homer gave the Royals a 4–2 lead, a score that would stand for the final margin. A sweep? Yes. An easy one? No. But what a reward for a team that had been on the brink of the World Series since losing on a homer in the bottom of the ninth inning in Game Five of the 1976 ALCS.

The Royals' George Brett is congratulated in the dugout after hitting a home run against the New York Yankees in Game 1 of the 1980 ALCS in Kanas City. After losing to the Yankees in the ALCS from 1976 to 1978, Brett helped lead the Royals to a three-game sweep of their rivals, and a spot in the World Series for the first time in team history. (Courtesy *Baseball Hall of Fame*)

"It was easy to get over that one," Brett said. "It was pretty easy. It was our first time in it. Then '77 was a lot harder and '78 was a lot harder. In '79, not making the playoffs was tough. In '80, beating them was tough, but what a thrill. We finally made it."

To finally clear the Yankee hurdle, the Royals relied upon submarine-style-throwing closer Dan Quisenberry. The right-handed Quisenberry got the win in Game Three, throwing 3 ⅔ innings in relief of Paul Splittorff, who pitched into the sixth and yielded just one run. Known simply as Quiz, the Royals closer finished games with regularity and ease—something the bullpen had lacked at times in previous years.

Known for his submarine style, Dan Quisenberry led the league in saves five times.
(Courtesy *Topeka Capital-Journal*)

"As soon as Quisenberry came around, we started winning in the playoffs," Brett said.

Quisenberry came up in July 1979 and pitched in 32 games. In his first full season in the majors in 1980, Quisenberry led the league in appearances (75) and saves (33). Quisenberry went 12-7 that year and pitched 128 ⅓ innings. Quisenberry also won the first of his five AL Rolaids Relief Awards, the top honor given to a relief pitcher at the time.

"Back then, he was a guy you would give him the ball in the seventh and he would go to the ninth," Frank White said. "He was a guy that came in and said, 'I'm going to induce ground balls,' and we knew we had to make a play when he came in the game."

Unlike today's relievers, Quisenberry, the fun-loving jokester, didn't make his living with a 98 mph fastball.

"Most pitchers fear losing their fastball, but since I don't have one, I have nothing to fear," Quisenberry once said.

So Quisenberry pitched with a sinker, and once in a while a curveball just to change it up. At top speed Quisenberry could hit the low-to-mid-80s on the radar gun. So instead of velocity, he relied on consistency. His control was pinpoint, and his sinker was at times unhittable.

With Quisenberry, who was signed as an undrafted free agent, the Royals finally found the relief they had been looking for. And when he struck out Willie Randolph for the final out in the ALCS, the Royals were in the World Series for the first time.

For Dennis Leonard, beating the Yankees was especially gratifying. From 1976 to 1978, Leonard started six games against the Yankees in the playoffs and was a tough-luck 1-3. But in Game Two of the 1980 ALCS, Leonard pitched eight innings of two-run ball, struck out eight, and was the winning pitcher, while Quisenberry got the save.

Later in his career, Leonard would battle knee and finger injuries, so 1980 turned out to be the only time he got play in a World Series, making that three-game sweep of the Yankees really stand out.

"I always thank 1980 because if my whole career went by and we never beat the Yankees in the playoffs, it would have been total frustration," Leonard said. "But finally we did beat them in '80, we swept them and had the first opportunity to put a team into the World Series."

White was named ALCS MVP after hitting .545 with a home run and three RBIs.

"In '78, that wasn't as classic of a playoff series as the first two, but 1980 I think was the year that our guys felt the most pressure because we had another shot," White said. "It was the Yankees again, and people were saying that we can't let these guys do it again. Three times is enough, and the players felt that pressure. Then we went on to sweep the Yankees in three games.

"In a lot of the guys' minds we just said, 'OK, we lost three straight playoffs. Now we got the first two games at home, let's win them and let's go to New York and take one and let's go to the World Series.'"

World of Disappointment

Similar to the Royals, the Philadelphia Phillies lost in the NLCS from 1976 to 1978 and missed the playoffs in 1979. But when the two teams met in the 1980

World Series, there was little doubt in the Royals' mind just who the better team was.

The Royals were up 4-0 in Game One in Philadelphia, led 4-2 in Game Two, and led 3-2 in Game Five, but their bullpen, which had been stellar all season, faltered, and the Phillies won all three games and ultimately the Series in six games. Phillies third baseman Mike Schmidt, the 1980 NL MVP, also took home World Series MVP honors, hitting two home runs to go with six RBIs.

In Game One, Amos Otis hit a two-run home run in the second inning, and Willie Aikens hit a two-run homer in the third, to stake the Royals to a 4-0 lead. But the Phillies touched Dennis Leonard for five runs in the third and another in the fourth. The Phillies eventually scored seven straight to take a 7-4 advantage, but the final margin was closer, as Aikens hit another two-run homer in the eighth.

In Game Two, facing ace Steve Carlton, the Royals scored once in the sixth and three in the seventh, but a four-run Phillies' eighth—two charged to Larry Gura and two to Dan Quisenberry—proved to be the Royals' downfall in a 6-4 defeat. Game Two also is remembered for something else. George Brett removed himself from the game in the sixth inning with hemorrhoids. He underwent minor surgery that night and returned for Game Three back in Kansas City.

In Game Three, with all his troubles behind him, Brett homered to give the Royals the lead in the first inning, and Otis's blast in the seventh gave the Royals a 3-2 lead. In the eighth, Pete Rose's single tied it at 3-3, but the Royals won it in the tenth, as Aikens' hit to deep center against closer Tug McGraw scored Willie Wilson for the game-winner.

The momentum carried over in Game Four as the Royals evened things with a 5-3 victory. Aikens hit two home runs, Leonard threw seven quality innings, and Quisenberry got the save. In Game Five, Otis's third home run of the World Series tied it at 2-2 in the sixth, and three batters later, UL Washington's sac fly gave the Royals a 3-2 lead. But Quisenberry gave up two runs in the ninth.

In Game Six, the Phillies won 4-1, scoring twice in the third and adding runs in the fifth and sixth to take a commanding 4-0 lead with Carlton on the mound. John Wathan scored for the Royals in the eighth, but that was as close as they would get, as McGraw struck out Wilson to end it. But Aikens believes the best team didn't win.

"I'll always feel that way," Aikens said.

Though Aikens hit four homers and had five RBIs, and Brett hit .375, the Royals couldn't get the key hit they needed. But like Aikens, White still believes the Royals should have been champions.

"The thing that bothered me about that whole series was after it was all over not a lot of people talked about how we could have won that series and that we should have won that series," White said. "But a lot of people talked about how we swept the Yankees, and how that was our World Series. But I think it just went to 'OK, what's the lesser of two evils?'"

Though the 1980 season ended on a sour note, there was still plenty to celebrate. The team won 97 games, Wilson stole 79 bases and led the league in hits with 230, and Brett signed a contract extension. Brett's decision to remain a Royal had little to do with money. Instead, it had everything to do with returning to the World Series.

"That's one of the reasons I'd keep signing five-year contracts, because I didn't want to go play elsewhere," Brett said. "Granted, I could have made more money in LA or Texas, or whoever was buying free agents at that time. But I didn't see them playing in October, and I saw us playing in October. And to me, baseball is a lot of fun in April, May, June, and July. But it's *a lot* of fun in October.

"That's when you go to bed, and you're heart's beating fast, and you get up in the morning, and you're heart starts beating faster."

Part Two

6

Royal Highness

A Yankee Becomes a Royal

George Steinbrenner had a habit of firing managers. So it's really no surprise the Yankees owner let Dick Howser go after the Yankees were swept by the Royals in the 1980 ALCS.

The Yankees went 103-59 in the regular season in Howser's only season at the helm. In most places, that's enough to get you a contract extension, but not in New York and certainly not with "The Boss." Officially, the Yankees said Howser resigned to pursue business opportunities, but the only business Howser wanted to manage was a baseball team.

The day before the official announcement that Howser wouldn't return to the Yankees, he called his twin daughters, Jana and Jill, and gave the two college girls a heads-up.

"He had said to us that I've had an incredibly long career in this game, something for which I am grateful for the rest of my life," recalled Jana, who serves as

Dick Howser is widely considered the Royals' greatest manager of all time. Howser managed the team from 1981 to 1986 and won 404 games. (Courtesy *Topeka Capital-Journal*)

executive vice president for the College Baseball Hall of Fame and works to uphold her dad's legacy. "But he had considered at that point—the point of being fired by the Yankees—that he was very grateful for all his years as a player, coach, and manager and he was going to consider himself retired."

But on August 30, 1981, Howser was hired by the Royals. Like with New York, Howser had a history with Kansas City. He was signed by the A's in 1958 and was an All-Star shortstop and Rookie of the Year in 1961 when he hit .280 and stole 37 bases. Howser played parts of his first three seasons in Kansas City before being traded to Cleveland in 1963. He played four seasons with the Indians before playing his last two with the Yankees.

Howser then spent ten years as the third-base coach for the Yankees and won two World Series rings as a coach with the team. In 1979, he returned to his alma mater and coached at Florida State. Howser, who grew up in West Palm Beach, wasn't recruited much out of high school but made the team at a tryout and graduated in four years. While at Florida State, he also got to spend time with childhood friend Burt Reynolds, who was on the football team.

While in the A's organization, Howser met his first wife, who was from Kansas City, and she still had family in the area when he became Royals manager. Upon taking the job, Howser again called his daughters.

"We were over-the-moon excited that he was coming back to Kansas City," Jana said. "And he was excited enough to say, 'I'm unretired, I'm not going to be done with baseball, and I'm going back to Kansas City.' That's the only time we remember where he changed the course based on what he had said before.

"The key was because of the ownership of Ewing Kauffman and the type of men that both he and John Schuerholz were."

Though Joe Burke hired Howser, Schuerholz was promoted to GM in October, and Howser had some say in player personnel during his time as manager.

"Our dad was back in Kansas City, and it was an incredibly wonderful time," Jana said. "But the full-circle nature of it is something every day that I think about because it speaks to the aspirations of dreams and keeping our eye on what's most important."

During a baseball career that spanned twenty-five years, Howser made a name for himself as a player and coach, but it was as a manager where he excelled the most.

"He was the epitome of the saying, 'Never let them see you sweat,'" Frank White said. "And he may have been churning on the inside, but he never showed it on the outside. And whenever a situation looked like it was going to be difficult, he would be the one that would say, 'Piss on it, guys. We're going to get it done.' And I think that is the attitude that he brought to our club.

"And we always knew he had the winning attitude from being with the Yankees, and he was used to being around veteran guys and used to winning. And all these things played out well for us when he came to Kansas City."

A quiet leader, stoic and fearless, even when he later battled brain cancer, Howser's Royals teams never finished lower than second and made the playoffs three times, including 1981, when he guided the team to a 20-13 finish, essentially running away with the second-half title.

Because of a midseason strike, the season was split in two, and the winners of each half (before and after the strike) met in the first round of the playoffs, creating an extra tier in the postseason. The Royals played the A's in the first round and were swept 3-0. But the Royals were back to being the Royals.

Under Howser, the Royals became aggressive again on the bases, much like they had done when Whitey Herzog was in the dugout. But there were differences between Howser and Herzog.

"Dick was more quiet and laid back," George Brett said. "If we'd get in a bad rut, Whitey would yell and scream. You'd get in a rut with Dick, he'd say, 'Piss on it. We'll get it done, don't panic.' Dick was more even-tempered, and Whitey was more up and down. But I got along with both of them extremely well."

With Howser at the helm, the Royals enjoyed a string of success, going 404-365 in parts of six seasons with him in the dugout. On the field, Howser is best known for taking the franchise to a new level, but he also is remembered for being taken far too soon.

The Pine Tar Game

"You play baseball for 20 years and you're always going to be remembered for one thing."
—*George Brett*

Only July 24, 1983, something controversial, remarkable, and unforgettable took place at Yankee Stadium. The Royals were trailing 4-3 in the top of the ninth inning, and Yankees closer Goose Gossage was on the mound looking for the final out. To the plate stepped George Brett, and with UL Washington at first, Brett represented the go-ahead run.

Gossage vs. Brett.

Power vs. power.

Royals vs. Yankees.

Does it get any better than that?

Yes.

Brett hammered a Gossage fastball into the seats in right field, giving the Royals a 5-4 lead. That alone really isn't that impressive, but what transpired after has become one of the most memorable scenes in baseball history.

When Brett scored, Yankees manager Billy Martin was already on the field conferring with home plate umpire Tim McClelland. Martin wanted him to check the bat, believing Brett had too much pine tar. In the dugout, Brett received congratulations from teammates and watched as the umpiring crew examined his bat.

The rulebook says no substance of any kind can be more than 18 inches from the tip of the bat. So as Brett sat in the dugout, he was somewhat confused about what was going on. He thought they might be checking for a corked bat, but Brett never had to use a corked bat to get a hit, so that couldn't be it.

Frank White then leaned in with clarification, telling Brett that the umpires were checking to see if he had too much pine tar. White also told Brett that the odds did not favor the Royals, since Dick Howser was still in the dugout and Martin was still on the field.

"If they call me out, I'm going to kill one of those SOBs," Brett said.

McClelland laid the bat across home plate, which is 17 inches wide. He then picked up the bat and pointed it at Brett.

Out!

An enraged Brett charged out of the dugout, his eyes wide, his arms flailing, his mouth moving as fast as his legs, which quickly carried him to within an inch of McClelland.

"When the umpire made the decision that George was out at the time, you just see the passion that Brett showed was in that call," White said. "And it showed how bad we wanted to beat the Yankees, and I think it all came out in that one play in that one instance."

Brett, of course, had to be restrained. Second-base umpire Joe Brinkman was the first to corral Brett, eventually putting him in a headlock. In a flash, Howser also ran onto the field and gave McClelland a piece of his mind. Amid the chaos, Howser threw his hat, and Gaylord Perry took the bat and ran up the tunnel. All the while, Howser's daughter Jana was watching on TV.

"I did see the whole entire thing unfold, and I'm sure my eyes were like saucers as it all was happening," she said. "It was just the convergence of a whole lot of circumstances and history. I do think my dad really believed George had done nothing wrong, which is why when it started to escalate that he was so fervent about it because he didn't think George had done anything wrong. And here he had been a coach alongside Billy Martin, and they had known each other for years. And I think it was a perfect storm."

Back on the field, Royals backup infielder Greg Pryor was making his way in from the bullpen after Brett was ruled out. Since Howser had both his catchers in the game—Don Slaught behind the plate and John Wathan at first—he had sent Pryor out to catch Don Hood, who was warming up in the ninth.

Hood played ten years in the majors and finished his career with 364 walks and 374 strikeouts, and Pryor had never been in the bullpen until that day.

"I go out to the bullpen, and I'm warming up Don Hood, who was wild as heck," Pryor said. "And I was saying, 'Man, I'm glad I've never done this and I'll never do this. This is terrible!' This guy's bouncing balls off your chin and wherever. So I was out in the bullpen watching this home run off George Brett's bat go into the right field stands from afar, from the bullpen. And I was so excited and we all stopped. All of the sudden, I saw the bustling from around home plate, and I knew exactly what was going on because I had a minor league manager pull that on me in A-ball one time for thinking I had too much pine tar.

"When I saw them lay the bat down, I thought he had no chance. And then George ran out, and we were all watching from the bullpen, and the game was over because he was the third out. So we slowly took all of our stuff and walked across left field, right past the monuments, and went back into the dugout."

In the clubhouse, Pryor's locker was next to Brett's, and there were reporters everywhere waiting for Brett. So Pryor sat down next to Hal McRae's locker and drank a beer and waited until the media left. Then he walked over to Brett.

"Hey, what are you upset about?" Pryor asked.

"What do you mean?" Brett said. "I lost a homer, we lost the game."

"Look at the bright side," Pryor responded. "There's a company that makes pine tar that's going to come to you for an endorsement. You're going to make so much money to endorse their pine tar."

Brett then smiled.

"What a great idea," Brett said. "I'm in a good mood now. We're going to go eat!"

Looking back at that day, Brett still smiles.

"I was laughing that night," Brett said. "I wasn't laughing when it happened. It wasn't funny. But then forty minutes later, or an hour later when we were getting on the bus, I was laughing my ass off with the guys on the team."

The Yankees and Royals had played in Kansas City a week earlier, and Martin had noticed all the pine tar on Brett's bat. Thinking it might be an illegal bat, Martin waited for the right opportunity to make his case. That opportunity didn't present itself in Kansas City, but a homer by Brett in the top of the ninth at Yankee Stadium was the perfect backdrop.

"It wasn't a spur-of-the-moment thing," said Steve Balboni, who played first base for the Yankees that day until Don Mattingly hit for him in the seventh inning. "They [the coaches] had seen the bat. George, he didn't use batting gloves, he just used pine tar, and the donut went way to the top of his bat, which brought the pine tar way up there. So it wasn't him putting it on trying to cheat or anything, it's just that's the way the bat looked.

"Everyone [in the Yankees clubhouse] was happy, obviously. But we kind of knew it was going to happen. I mean, you kind of felt bad for George losing a home run, but it was us winning."

Except it wasn't. The Royals appealed the ruling, and four days later AL President Lee MacPhail overruled the umpire's decision, saying pine tar did not help Brett hit the ball over the fence, and that the game had to be resumed.

The Pine Tar Game resumed August 18 at a rather empty Yankee Stadium. Brett did not accompany the team, but Martin still had tricks up his sleeve. When the Yankees took the field, Martin had the left-handed Mattingly play second and pitcher Ron Guidry in center. And before the first pitch, Martin tried to appeal to the new umpiring crew that Brett did not touch all the bases. Martin, however, was outfoxed. The crew came prepared, showing Martin a sworn affidavit from the previous crew stating that Brett had in fact touched all four bases.

Dan Quisenberry retired the Yankees in order, and the Royals won 5-4. Finally order had been restored. But the Royals slipped down the stretch and finished that season 79-83. Maybe Brett should have kept the bat.

After the incident on July 24, Brett used the bat for a couple more games. He was quite fond of it because it had fewer grains in the wood, which made it harder. But Perry told Brett that he was playing with an expensive piece of lumber, and Brett then sold it to a collector for $25,000. He soon realized his mistake and bought it back and donated it to the Hall of Fame.

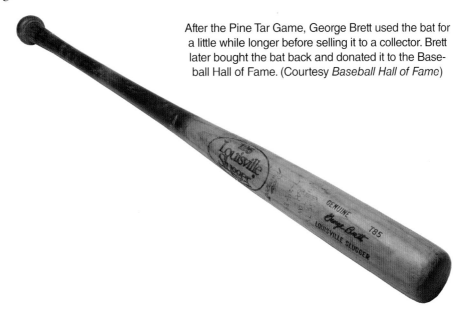

After the Pine Tar Game, George Brett used the bat for a little while longer before selling it to a collector. Brett later bought the bat back and donated it to the Baseball Hall of Fame. (Courtesy *Baseball Hall of Fame*)

Part Two

The announced attendance for the Pine Tar Game was 33,944. But millions of baseball fans young and old have seen it, making the image of Brett running out of the dugout no doubt a lasting memory.

"For me to be remembered as that, I think it's awesome," Brett said.

Prelude to a Championship

In 1984, Bret Saberhagen, Mark Gubicza, and Danny Jackson arrived at spring training in Fort Myers, Florida, a little wide-eyed. The three were rookie pitchers trying to play their way onto a veteran team, and they made a pretty solid first impression on George Brett.

"You're like, 'God damn! These guys are pretty good,'" Brett said. "The next thing you know they make the team."

Far different from today's game, the '80s were a time when rookies tried to avoid talking to the manager. Gubicza and Saberhagen fit in with the times.

"Back then if you made the team the manager didn't tell you anything," Gubicza said. "If you avoided a conversation with the manager that means you had a chance to make the team. I remember Sabes and I sneaking our luggage in there when we were flying off to Memphis not really knowing, and George said, 'Hey, by the way, you both are living with me.'

"I was like, 'Wow!' I remember calling home eventually from George's house after a while waiting to use the phone—that was pre–cell phone—and telling my parents that not only I made the big leagues, but I'm staying with George Brett. And they were out of their minds. My brothers were going nuts and it was really an amazing thing to bring us in. A lot of times veteran guys just keep the youngsters aside. It's a little different nowadays where you feel comfortable right away, but back then you were like, 'Yes, sir.' And you better do everything they asked you to do as far as taking their luggage out and all that jazz."

The Royals opened the 1984 season with a homestand against the Yankees and Indians, and Gubicza was the team's fourth starter. In the Yankees series, the Royals PA announcer broadcast the pitching matchups for the Cleveland series, but the announcer butchered the pronunciation of Gubicza's last name—one of "a gazillion times" Gubicza estimated that happened during his career.

Gubicza was in the dugout at the time, and near Dick Howser, the manager he was somewhat scared to talk to. After hearing the name gaffe, Howser grabbed the phone and called upstairs to the press box. According to Gubicza, the conversation went like this.

"You tell that blankety-blank-blank to get his name right!" Gubicza said, recalling how Howser shouted into the phone. "We got a kid making his major league debut for God's sake!"

After that, Gubicza said he was more at ease around Howser knowing he had his back. In 1984, the Royals also acquired first baseman Steve Balboni from the Yankees.

"It was really hard because all I knew were the Yankees, and I really loved it there, so I didn't really want to leave," Balboni said. "But I knew to get an opportunity to play I was going to need to leave so it was mixed feelings. But Dick Howser called me, and after talking to him I was really excited about going over.

"He had known me from his days with the Yankees, and he was the one that was responsible for getting me over there. And he made me feel real comfortable and real welcome, and after I talked to him I was excited about coming."

That season, the Royals won the division but lost to the Tigers three straight in the playoffs. Detroit went on to defeat San Diego in the World Series. The Tigers started the season 35-5, and one of those loses came against Saberhagen, the twenty-year-old who was about to lead the Royals to the top.

The I-70 Series

It's about 250 miles from Kansas City to St. Louis, but on October 26, 1985, one step, and a blown call, turned the World Series on its head.

It was the bottom of the ninth inning in Game Six at Kauffman Stadium. The Royals trailed 1-0 on the scoreboard and were down 3-2 in the series and just three outs from sadness when pinch-hitter Jorge Orta stepped in to face Cardinals closer Todd Worrell.

Orta hit a squibber to the right side, and Cardinals first baseman Jack Clark fielded and flipped to Worrell at the bag. Worrell extended his left arm for the ball,

Part Two

The 1985 World Series featured a "Show Me State" matchup between the Kansas City Royals and the St. Louis Cardinals. That's Bret Saberhagen throwing a pitch in Game Seven, an 11-0 Royals win. Saberhagen threw a complete-game shutout and was named MVP. (Courtesy *Baseball Hall of Fame*)

and Orta extended his right leg, lunging for the base. First-base umpire Don Denkinger swiped both arms and declared Orta safe—a controversial declaration that would be proven incorrect. Replays showed Orta was out by a step, and Cardinals fans would soon come to despise Denkinger, the call, and the Royals.

Steve Balboni then hit a pop foul near the Royals first-base dugout. Clark lost track of the ball and it bounced over his head, giving Balboni, who was a giant in those days at 6-foot-3 and 225 pounds, another crack. Balboni then singled, and the Royals had two on with no outs. Onix Concepcion ran for Balboni, and catcher Jim Sundberg bunted into a fielder's choice as Worrell threw Orta out at third. After a passed ball, Worrell intentionally walked Hal McRae to bring up backup infielder Dane Iorg.

Iorg hit a blooper to right, and Andy Van Slyke, who had one of the best arms in the game, made a perfect throw home. But Sundberg made a perfect slide to beat the tag, and the Royals won 2-1. Bret Saberhagen's son Drew was born that day, and one night later Saberhagen threw a complete-game shutout, lifting the Royals to an easy 11-0 win in Game Seven, giving the Royals their first World Series title, and making them the first team in history to win the World Series after losing the first two games at home.

Before the final out in Game Seven, George Brett went over to Saberhagen and gave an order.

"You come party with me," Brett told the twenty-one-year-old phenom who was named World Series MVP.

After right fielder Darryl Motley, who started the rout with a two-run homer in the second inning, caught the final out, Saberhagen leaped into the arms of Brett—an iconic moment in Royals history.

"It was probably the happiest I've ever been with a uniform on in my life," said Brett, who hit .370 in the World Series.

That moment wouldn't have been possible if not for Brett, who willed his team to victory in Game Three of the ALCS against Toronto after the Royals had dropped the first two games of the series. In Game Three, Brett went 4-for-4 with two home runs and three RBIs in a 6-5 victory. The Royals then won the series in seven games.

Brett's performance in Game Three was the best of his career in a career filled with games that would be considered the best for many. But October is when players are remembered most, and that is certainly the case for Brett.

Saberhagen also falls into that category. After falling behind 2-0 in the Series to the Cardinals, he pitched nine innings of one-run ball and struck out eight in Game Three, lifting the Royals to a 6-1 win.

Royals third baseman George Brett hit .370 against the St. Louis Cardinals in the 1985 World Series. (Courtesy *Baseball Hall of Fame*)

Saberhagen's victory in Game Three also marked a first for Royals manager Dick Howser. It was the first time he won a game as a manager in a World Series.

For the trip to St. Louis, the Howser family didn't go with the team. Instead, they piled into Howser's conversion van and made the drive down I-70, even stopping for ice cream.

"It was a peaceful, quieter time to just spend with family," said his daughter Jana. "My dad had a pretty cool conversion van, a very nice one. And we just decided to drive. I remember him saying that between driving to the airport and flying over and getting all the equipment and getting to the hotel, we could get there in the same amount of time so let's drive. It was that simple."

Frank White became the first second baseman to hit cleanup in the Series since Jackie Robinson in 1952, and White hit a towering home run off Joaquin Andujar in Game Three. In 1985, White hit 22 home runs in the regular season and had a homer and six RBIs in the World Series.

"Dick was a guy that I really, really admired because when he came to Kansas City from the Yankees, he was the one manager that really saw in me more than just a glove," White said. "He saw a guy who in the right spot could generate some offense.

"So if he hadn't seen the promise in me as an offensive player, and given me the opportunity, I wouldn't have been able to accomplish a lot of those things that I was able to accomplish."

The Royals lost Game Four and were down 3-1 in the Series before coming back. What propelled them to rally in both the ALCS and World Series is the same thing that helped them come back from being seven games back at the All-Star break.

"We had a good, young nucleus of guys, and it was kind of a family," Saberhagen said of the 1985 team.

One such occasion where the family all showed up was when Balboni had a birthday party for his two-year-old son in spring training.

"When you're in a little apartment, you don't have room," said Balboni, who hit a Royals' single-season-record 36 homers that season. "You don't expect everyone to show up, but they did. And that's the kind of team we were."

And White believes the 1985 team—not the 1977 team—was the best of his era.

"You have guys who said '85 wasn't our best team," White said. "In '77 we had a really good team, but it's hard to say that the team that won the World Series wasn't your best team."

General manager John Schuerholz massaged the roster throughout the season, and there were plenty of unsung heroes. In January, Schuerholz acquired Sundberg from the Brewers, and in May he acquired left fielder Lonnie Smith from the Cardinals. Another key contributor was shortstop Buddy Biancalana.

Biancalana was a career .199 hitter prior to the 1985 season, but his name became a household name thanks in part to David Letterman. In August of that year, Letterman started a hit counter comparing Biancalana's career mark to Pete Rose's.

In 1985, Biancalana hit just .188 during the regular season, but the fan favorite hit .278 in the World Series and played solid defense. He also went on Letterman's show after the World Series.

"From a notoriety standpoint, geez, one week of playing in the World Series, and playing pretty well, and the opportunities that arose from it was very, very life changing," Biancalana said. "I always say that it was an umpire's bad call that changed my life."

The call also changed other lives, with the loss in Game Six serving as a death blow to the Cardinals in Game Seven. But to be fair, no team probably could have overcome that ending in Game Six.

"If we would have had instant replay, we would have been world champions. Well, it's thirty years too late," Whitey Herzog said with a chuckle. "I don't want to sound like sour grapes. Their starting pitching just shut us down. We didn't have (Vince) Coleman, he got run over by the tarp (Coleman was injured in the NLDS when his leg was caught under the automatic tarpaulin prior to Game Four at Busch Stadium and missed the Series) and he was a catalyst. They shut us down. Our base stealers never got on base."

After the final out, Howser tucked his hat under his jacket and ran onto the field and celebrated with his team. Jana later stopped by his office. She was attending college in California at the time and got the OK from her professors to go to Kansas City and experience the World Series with her family.

Jana still has all seven tickets framed where she can see them every day, a reminder of "an incredible once-in-a-lifetime chance to see that history happening." As she looked at her dad, now a World Series champion, she saw something that she'll never forget.

"I remember the look on his face, the look in his eyes that everything about what he loved about baseball had come true," she said. "You see the sense of great satisfaction after decades of hard work and teamwork and what it takes to do that as a team, and I have kept that with me all of this time because I could see that it meant so much to him.

"And I know that for the rest of his life—he wasn't proud of himself—he was proud of his team and all the people that coached with and played for him because he believed in them, and that's the key. He believed in his people with all his heart."

PART THREE

ROYAL PAIN

7

The End of an Era

Part Three

The Worst and Best Trade

David Cone was a prankster. But on March 27, 1987, Cone was convinced the joke was on him. When general manager John Schuerholz told Cone that he had been traded to the Mets, Cone's heart sunk, and he could barely stand.

"I was obviously floored by it," Cone said. "I thought it was a joke. John Schuerholz told me I was traded, and he kept talking, and I said, 'Please, just give me a minute.' It was hard to process what he had just told me. I was in shock."

Cone was the native son, drafted by the Royals in the third round in 1981 as a pitcher out of Rockhurst High School, a private Catholic school in Kansas City. He was one of the game's best up-and-coming prospects, and as a die-hard Royals fan growing up, Cone dreamed of playing in All-Star Games and winning a World Series with his hometown team.

Cone said Billy Gardner, who was filling in for a then-terminally ill Dick Howser, had "kind of insinuated" that he would be the team's fifth starter out of spring training, so Cone felt he had nothing to worry about.

The Royals believed Ed Hearn would be their catcher of the future, but he played in just 13 games for the ballclub as injuries and illness ended his career. (Courtesy *Topeka Capital-Journal*)

Cone was just twenty-four at the time of the trade that sent him and catcher Chris Jelic to the Mets in exchange for top catching prospect Ed Hearn and pitchers Rick Anderson and Mauro Gozzo. The trade, at least on paper, had *some* merit.

The Royals were stocked with pitching and were looking for a good, young catcher, as Jim Sundberg was already gone and Jamie Quirk and Larry Owen weren't really considered everyday players. Hearn, though he had spent eight years in the minors, was still just twenty-six at the time. And the Mets were coming off a World Series championship in 1986 in which he filled in admirably for Gary Carter behind the plate.

Hearn wasn't totally surprised when the trade was announced. He had heard rumors of his name floating around with the Royals since the winter of '86, but since the deal was made so late in spring training, it caught him off guard.

"It was kind of a double-edged sword," Hearn said. "I felt like the Mets were stacked with talent, and they had just come off that World Series win. And I was feeling like there could be a run and there could be some very good opportunities to win some more rings. But I think we all play the game to be a starting player and once you're in the game, your goal is to stay in the game. And that's usually as a starting player and nobody likes sitting on the bench.

"So I was really looking forward to it, especially because the Royals had a really good pitching staff. And they were young, and one of my strengths was handling pitching staffs. And I was a perfect fit, as far as I was concerned."

The Royals called Cone up to the big leagues in June 1986. He pitched in 11 games out of the bullpen that season, going 0-0 with a 5.56 ERA. He was looking forward to getting his first win as a Royal, but that obviously didn't happen.

"I thought I was finally going to get my chance," Cone said. "Even though I had my debut here in '86—I did make it here—I did make it to the big leagues here and that was something I'll never forget. So obviously the next spring in '87 was when I thought I would get my shot and be part of the rotation."

Instead, Cone eventually became a valued member of the Mets rotation that was led by Dwight Gooden. In his first season with the Mets, Cone started 13 games and pitched out of the bullpen eight times. In 1988, Cone became an All-Star and went 20-3.

Cone had never been to New York until the trade, and living in the Big Apple and playing with the party-hard Mets was quite an adjustment for the Midwestern-raised Cone.

"I was thrown right into the lot with the '86 world champion Mets, who were a wild group of guys," Cone said. "It was eye-opening without a doubt. I did everything I could to fit in, and I kind of became a wild guy just to fit in with that group.

"Now I've learned how to adapt. I've learned how to navigate myself around New York, where to live. It's really challenging, even just the off-the-field stuff like finding a place to live, driving, finding your way around. There's so much to deal with. And, of course, the media, as well. There's so much attention and scrutiny, and that part was eye-opening."

While Cone became one of the NL's best pitchers, Hearn's troubles began shortly after arriving at Royals camp. He started the first two games of the season and had four hits in six at-bats but soon went on the DL with a torn rotator cuff, and his season was over after just six games. In 1988, Hearn played in just seven games, and just like that his career was over.

The throw-ins in the deal didn't fare much better. Anderson played in 13 games with the Royals and was out of baseball by 1989. Gozzo never played for the Royals and won seven games in parts of six seasons in the big leagues, and Jelic played four games for the Mets in 1990.

For Hearn, the worst thing that happened to him during his professional career was a simple baseball trade that didn't work out. But in the game of life, he has endured much more.

During a routine physical in 1991, Hearn was diagnosed with focal segmental glomerulosclerosis, a degenerative kidney disease that forced him on dialysis. He subsequently had three kidney transplants. He also battled skin cancer, and mood swings and depression were two of the side effects of the medication he was taking.

One day, Hearn went down to the basement of his home in Shawnee, Kansas, a suburb of Kansas City, and stared down the barrel of a loaded .357 Magnum. Hearn wanted to pull the trigger. But he couldn't.

"That day, it was very clear to me," Hearn said. "I had a wonderful wife and I had a great upbringing so I had a foundation. Even though I was contemplating quitting on things, when you have a strong foundation, it's like a house. Strong foundations and things that are built on strong materials are going to hold up. And I think that was a big part of what allowed me to get through that day."

Before Hearn left the basement, he promised himself to be more proactive in three ways with his faith.

"Listening to the coach, talking to the coach, and reading the playbook—the Bible," Hearn said. "I kind of got away from that the previous couple years. And then you got to hang out with good people that have like values who will not only support you but also hold you accountable for your life."

Hearn also got professional help, and he began reading more. He now has quite a collection of self-help books and biographies. While in the basement, though, Hearn's life took another twist. He recalled the advice from renowned motivational speaker Zig Ziglar, whom he had heard speak previously.

"You can change where you're at in life by what you put into your mind," Hearn remembered Ziglar saying to him. Hearn then began a new career as a public speaker. For more than twenty years, Hearn has traveled the country telling others his story of tragedy and triumph, and today he is one of the nation's most sought-after public speakers.

Over the years, Hearn has received many letters from people saying that he saved their lives. And some have told him that they believe the David Cone trade was the best trade the Royals ever made.

"I think from a pure baseball standpoint it's a ridiculously lopsided trade," Hearn said. "But I don't think that a lot people go, 'Ed Hearn, he is so great, and he's better because what he's done since then.' But some people have told me that."

Death in the Royal Family

On the outfield concourse at Kauffman Stadium, just behind the fountains, there's a bronze statue of Dick Howser. His right foot is on the top step of the dugout, and he's wearing his famous Royals jacket and hat.

On the Royals Hall of Fame in left field, Howser's retired No. 10 is between George Brett's No. 5 and Frank White's No. 20, both honors a fitting tribute to the greatness of one man. Sometimes good people are taken way too soon. This was the case for Howser, who died at age fifty-one of brain cancer on June 17, 1987.

Howser's death shocked Kansas City and the baseball world. A beloved figure whose resolve helped lead the Royals to their first World Series title was gone not even two years later. Howser's death was tragic, and fast. Just a year earlier in 1986, Howser was managing the AL All-Star team in Houston. But that's when things took a turn for the worse.

In interviews prior to the game, Howser got some of the players' names confused. Howser said Lou Whitaker would start in left field, and Whitaker was Detroit's starting second baseman. He also referred to catcher Jim Sundberg as "Sabes," the nickname for Royals pitcher Bret Saberhagen.

"I knew he was having problems," said the Cardinals' Whitey Herzog, who was manager of the NL All-Stars. "He and I did a show for the press the night before, and when he came out to home plate for the All-Star Game, he didn't have a lineup card so I knew there was something seriously wrong.

"I told the umpire, 'Don't say nothing. I'll have one of my coaches write it up and give it to you.' So I did. He was a wonderful person, he really was. He did a good job. He was a people person and he could handle his men very well."

Howser's daughter Jana was in college that summer in California and was in the process of transferring to UMKC, so she didn't attend the game. But watching it on TV, she became concerned.

"I recognized that he didn't look like himself," she said. "And as soon as that started with him being confused about who the players were—that was not in the realm of possibility with his normal function and normalcy in his life. He knew who everybody was. So I knew something was very, very wrong.

"By the end of the game, that very night, he descended rapidly. And he was flown back to Kansas City that night after the game, and as I understand, he flew back on the Kauffmans' plane."

The All-Star Game was the last game Howser ever managed, a 3-2 win by the AL. Frank White hit a home run in the seventh inning, which proved to be the decisive run.

Manager Dick Howser led the Royals to their first World Series title in 1985, but sadly he died two years later. After his death, Howser's No. 10 was the first number to be retired in Royals history. (Courtesy *Baseball Hall of Fame*)

Back in Kansas City, Howser was admitted to St. Luke's Hospital, and doctors later found a malignant tumor in his brain. He underwent surgery, and a portion of the golf ball–sized tumor was removed from his left frontal lobe. Howser then underwent weeks of radiation.

"Once there was a diagnosis there were no discussions of long, long-term survival with the type of illness that he had," Jana said. "So I saw him very, very frequently. He was being taken care of at St. Luke's, I was at UMKC, and to this day I cherish every one of those days that we had."

Mike Ferraro finished out the 1986 season as interim manager and was not retained. For a time, Howser showed some improvement, and there was hope he could manage the Royals again. But he had another surgery in December after doctors determined the tumor had grown. Still, Howser was in uniform when spring training began in 1987, but his body couldn't hold up, and he resigned two days later.

"My dad has the same qualities about him that was the never-ever-give-up attitude that yielded his wanting to come back and manage the team," Jana said. "And the Royals held his position. They did not permanently replace him nor did they even discuss anything like that until dad made the decision on his terms about what may or may not happen in his life. They gave him the arm's length to be treated, to try and get healthy, and to try and walk through the course of his illness in a way that he could with the great medical team around him and to ultimately arrive at a decision on his own. They felt that that should never come from anybody but my dad.

"At that spring training, he had lost a tremendous amount of weight and had gone through the surgeries and a lot of radiation and chemotherapy, and he was sick. And the combination of trying to do that, it all really is underlined by the fact that the Royals were never going to make that decision for him. And they wanted to treat him with absolutely dignity and respect. And I have a lifelong respect for the Royals and for the Kauffman family and John Schuerholz, and John knows this. He's a mentor and a dear friend for treating my dad with the proper respect that I feel a reigning World Series championship manager was due."

Howser's last public appearance was the Royals' 1987 home opener. Howser was inducted into the Royals Hall of Fame that July and his number was retired, becoming the first number to be retired in team history.

Howser's legacy is still felt today in Kansas City and across the country. Following his death, the Dick Howser Trophy—an award given to college baseball's top player based on athletics and academics—was established in 1987, and Florida State renamed its baseball field Dick Howser Stadium in his honor in 2005. He is buried in Tallahassee, Florida.

Part Three

Howser finished his Royals career with 404 wins, seven short of surpassing's Herzog's team record at the time. Howser was definitely one of the game's all-time greats. But sadly, his death was the first in a series of events that ultimately led to the downfall of the Royal kingdom. A tragedy, indeed.

The Ninth Gold Glove

Frank White won eight Gold Gloves during his eighteen seasons in the big leagues, but he actually has nine of them.

White won his first Gold Glove in 1977, beginning a stretch of winning the coveted award six seasons in a row through 1982. Detroit's Lou Whitaker won the honor from 1983 to 1985 before White reclaimed it the next two years.

In 1988, White played 148 games at second base. He committed a league-low four errors—all were throwing errors to four different first baseman. So White, at age thirty-seven, went the whole season without missing a ground ball, fly ball, or throw. Yet, despite having the best fielding percentage (.994) in the league and the fewest errors, he did not win the Gold Glove.

Seattle's Harold Reynolds won the award despite committing 18 errors. Had White won, he would have been the first second baseman in history to win nine Gold Gloves.

"It really was a unique year for me, but that would have really been the feather on the cap," White said. "And really the fans of Kansas City, they were as disappointed as I was so they had a big luncheon with a ninth Gold Glove of their own, which I though was pretty special coming from the fans."

That season, Reynolds had a .977 fielding percentage in ten more games and 71 more fielding chances than White, which was a factor in the 33-31 vote that was conducted by the league's managers and coaches. Still, it was no doubt one of the biggest snubs in history.

"He had one taken away," Art Stewart said.

White never got that chance again and retired in 1990, ending his career tied with Pittsburgh's Bill Mazeroski for what was then the most Gold Gloves ever by a second baseman. But for White, the Gold Gloves that he was awarded by MLB are indeed memorable, and two of them stand out the most.

"Probably the first and the last," White said. "Those are the ones you come in with and go out with."

On defense, White often smiled after robbing a player of a hit. He also had intelligence and used the lessons he learned from those he once played behind to his advantage.

"I think that when you first start playing, you're still trying to figure things out, and you're asking questions, and you're going to play in the winter leagues," White said. "I went to Venezuela two winters and went to Puerto Rico one winter just to fancy my trade and show that when Cookie (Rojas) retired I would be ready to step in and play second base.

"And Cookie always told me that when you learn when to do something and when not to do something, you're going to enjoy this game a lot more and what that meant was once you figure out how to play the game and make those decisions, you're going to enjoy the game a lot more and he was right about that."

In 1991, the Cubs' Ryne Sandberg passed White and Mazeroski for the most Gold Gloves by a second baseman with nine, and Roberto Alomar surpassed him in 2001 when he won his tenth, which is the most in MLB history. Sandberg, Mazeroski, and Alomar are in baseball's Hall of Fame. White, however, is not.

Voters looked down at White's career .255 batting average, but he was far from an automatic out, and his career numbers are nearly identical to Mazeroski's. Here's a look:

	GP	H	AVG.	HR	RBIs	FP	GG	ASG
Mazeroski	2,163	2,016	.260	138	853	.983	8	7
White	2,324	2,006	.255	160	886	.983	8	5

Though White is not in Cooperstown, he was elected to the Royals Hall of Fame in 1995, a fitting reward for a kid from Lincoln High School who helped build the stadium with his bare hands and became an icon in his hometown.

"I think what you do when you're a young player, and you're playing in the alleys and the backyard and the park, you're trying to emulate players that you hear on the radio and so forth," White said. "And I was blessed that I was able to grow up and go to school near old Municipal Stadium in Kansas City so I had a chance to see a lot of the A's play, and part of the dream about being a Major League Baseball player is when you get to a point where you got your feet planted firmly on a Major League Baseball field and having that feeling that you belong and you know how to handle to that situation, and then just the simple fact that I was able to play as long as I did, all those things come to mind.

"Then all those individual things you dream about as a kid like hitting a homer in the All-Star Game, hitting a home run in the World Series, winning a World Series, all those things ended up happening. That's what I thought about was all of those things as kid when I was realizing those goals."

The eight Gold Gloves White won are on display in the Royals Hall of Fame. But the ninth Gold Glove that he received from the fans? Well, that one's a keeper.

"I have it at home," White said. "It was well done. It showed me how much the fans were behind me. It was awesome."

Bo Knows Baseball

Sometimes ordinary men do extraordinary things. This never applied to Bo Jackson. He wasn't ordinary. He wasn't normal. Blessed with great speed and strength, he was extraordinary.

A standout running back at Auburn University, Jackson won the Heisman Trophy in 1985. The Tampa Bay Buccaneers had the first pick in the 1986 NFL Draft, and they flew Jackson in for a team visit in March. The flight was against NCAA rules, and Jackson was later ruled ineligible to play baseball halfway through his senior season.

As a junior, Jackson dominated for the Tigers, hitting .401 with 17 homers and 43 RBIs. But unable to complete his senior year, and upset by what transpired with the Buccaneers, Jackson warned the Bucs that if they drafted him, he would not sign. The Bucs drafted him anyway. True to his word, Jackson did not sign.

The Royals, however, believed they had a pretty good chance to sign Jackson, as scout Kenny Gonzales had been watching him for years and had become close to Jackson's family. Still, the Royals didn't think it made much sense to use one of their first three picks on Jackson given the fact that he was the best college football player in the nation and a pro football career wasn't out of the question. But Art Stewart, the team's scouting director at the time, figured a fourth-round pick was worth the gamble, so the Royals drafted Jackson 105th overall that June. A couple weeks later, Jackson signed with the Royals, turning down $7 million from the Bucs for a contract worth less than a million from the Royals.

"I went with what is in my heart," Jackson said when the deal was announced.

Several months earlier at the NFL combine, Jackson reportedly ran a 4.12 40-yard dash. Jackson—assigned to Double-A Memphis—made it to the big leagues nearly as fast. He made his Royals debut on September 2, 1986, thus beginning one of the most exciting (albeit brief) careers in professional sports. In his debut against the White Sox, Jackson hit a routine grounder to the second baseman. It turned out to be his first major league hit, as Jackson easily outran the throw to first.

Jackson's first home run came twelve days later—a 475-foot blast to left field, which is still the longest home run in Royals history.

"When Bo hit that, it took all the muscles off my body," said Royals backup infielder Greg Pryor, who was in the on-deck circle at the time.

With his baseball career on the fast track, Jackson reentered the 1987 NFL Draft, and the Raiders picked him in the seventh round. Once his baseball season was over, Jackson's "hobby" was suiting up in silver and black and running around, through, and over opposing defenders.

Already a two-sport star, Jackson became a worldwide marketing sensation with Nike's "Bo Knows" campaign that debuted in 1989. Millions of fans also found a new hobby in the late-'80s and early-'90s as they were glued to their TV sets playing Tecmo Bowl and Tecmo Super Bowl, with Jackson being perhaps the game's best player.

In 1989, Jackson, who scaled outfield walls and broke bats over his head and knee, gave Royals fans two of his many unbelievable moments. The first was The Throw. On June 5, Jackson and the Royals were playing in Seattle. It was the bottom of the tenth inning in a 3-3 game.

Seattle's Harold Reynolds was on first, and Scott Bradley hit a double to left. Reynolds was rounding third when Jackson picked up the ball near the warning track. Believing that Reynolds would score easily, Royals catcher Bob Boone had already started to leave the field. Then he saw a baseball flying in from more than 300 feet away.

Unaware of what was going on behind him, Reynolds, too, believed the game would be over soon. But he was surprised to see a teammate waving him to slide as there would be a play at the plate. Boone caught Jackson's strike and tagged out Reynolds, who threw his helmet in disbelief.

A month later at the All-Star Game in Anaheim, Jackson said hello. Batting leadoff for the AL, Jackson hit Rick Reuschel's second pitch 450 feet over the wall in center field. Royals pitcher Mark Gubicza joined Jackson on the AL roster, and when he came up, Gubicza thought something special could happen.

"That was right at the height of the 'Bo Knows' thing," Gubicza said." He was larger than life. It was like flying around with Mick Jagger and the Rolling Stones. I remember being in the bullpen, and I remember thinking that was a pretty good matchup for Bo. I was with a bunch of guys, Nolan Ryan was down there, and those guys were sitting there going, 'Why would it be a good matchup for Bo since Rueschel is a sinkerball pitcher?'

"And Bo, most right-hander batters are high-ball hitters, and lefties are low-ball hitters. Bo was just the opposite, and he crushed that sinker. You could hear that sound right off the bat, and the angle I had, I had no idea when, and if, it was

The Royals' Bo Jackson electrified baseball fans everywhere with his power, speed, and throwing ability. Here he is at the plate in 1989. (Courtesy *Baseball Hall of Fame*)

ever going to land. He absolutely crushed it and seeing the highlights down the road, and flying from Anaheim to New York to open up (the second half) and the onslaught of people that were following him around and going nuts, it was pretty cool."

After the 1990 season ended for the Royals, Jackson returned to what would be his final season of football. On January 13, 1991, the Raiders were playing the Bengals in a playoff game in Los Angeles. In the third quarter, Jackson took a pitch and ran up the right sideline. As defenders closed in, Jackson could have stepped out of bounds, but that wasn't his style. He cut back left and gained a few more yards before being tackled from behind.

At first, it looked like just a normal tackle. But Jackson initially didn't get up. He stayed down for a bit but eventually got to his feet. A few steps later, Jackson collapsed. He told team doctors that he thought he dislocated his left hip and it popped back into the socket—an unbelievable concept.

The injury was later described as a hip pointer, but it turned out Jackson was right. That winter, Jackson, who was still on crutches and unable to participate in spring training, met with Royals team physician Steve Joyce in Kansas City. It was later determined that Jackson had in fact dislocated his hip and he had a degenerative hip condition and would need a hip replacement. His football career was officially over at age twenty-eight, and his baseball career had been reduced to a question mark. The Royals then released Jackson in a cost-cutting move.

Jackson signed with the White Sox and played 23 games in 1991 before missing all of 1992 with hip surgery. He returned in 1993 and hit a homer in his first at-bat and finished his career with the Angels in 1994. More than twenty years later, former teammates still marvel at Jackson.

"He was probably the best athlete that I ever played with or ever saw," said Kevin Seitzer, who played for the Royals from 1986 to 1991. "He was really good."

"When he hit the ball, it sounded different than other people," said Pat Tabler, who played in KC from 1988 to 1990. "The things he did on the baseball field, I've never seen it done before, and I haven't seen it done since. The way he's running, the way he's throwing, the way he could hit. All the special things he would do on the field, it was almost like he was doing it, and he didn't know what he was doing. He was just doing it."

"Unfortunately he blew out his hip and was never the same player," George Brett said. "But he was a great teammate and a lot of fun to be a round. To this day, he's a great friend."

Part Three

Number 5 Goes 3-for-3

George Brett's legacy was already secure long before the 1990 season began. But he added to it by accomplishing something no other player in MLB history had done before.

With a .329 average in 1990, Brett became the first player to win batting titles in three different decades. Brett won his first batting title in 1976 when he hit .333 and won his second in 1980 when he hit .390. Brett said winning his third and final batting title was probably the most surprising compared to the other two for a number of reasons, starting with his age.

At thirty-seven, Brett was no longer a young man. And by 1990, he was starting to wind down an already exemplary career. The previous season, Brett hit .282, which was his lowest mark since his first full year in the big leagues in 1974.

In the first half of the 1990 season, Brett hit .267 with two homers, 12 doubles, and 29 RBIs—a far cry from the player who carried the Royals to a World Series title just five years earlier.

"I was hitting shitty at the break," Brett said. "I was hitting .250, .260 at the All-Star break, and everywhere we'd go, people in Boston, their columnist would write a story saying George Brett's lost it, this is probably his last year, and the Royals might eat his contract.

"We'd go to Chicago, and there'd be a columnist who would do a story on you and say the guy's over the hill, he can't play anymore. And then you'd go to New York, and you'd hear that, and you'd go to LA and you'd hear that. So you're looking at that the whole first half of the season."

Brett didn't have the numbers to make the All-Star Game, but he used the time off well.

"I just kind of hung out in Kansas City," Brett said. "I played some golf with some buddies, and I had some nice dinners and said, '(Screw) these guys. I'm going to prove them wrong.' I don't know what happened, but I got hot that second half. I don't know what I hit that second half, but I beat Rickey Henderson (Oakland) and Rafael Palmeiro (Texas) to win the batting championship."

Brett batted .388 after the All-Star break, hitting 12 home runs to go with 33 doubles and 58 RBIs in 71 games covering 278 at-bats. He hit .388 in July, .369 in August, and .396 in September and October.

Brett's ascent began the first game after the All-Star Game, when he went 3-for-5 with three doubles against Baltimore. He then hit for the cycle on July 25 at Toronto. In his first at-bat, Brett hit a sharp single to right. In his next at-bat, he tripled to center. Brett then ripped one down right-field line for a double before hitting a homer to center.

Brett had hit for the cycle once before against Baltimore on May 28, 1979, at Royals Stadium. When he accomplished the feat again in Toronto, he broke the MLB record for longest time between cycles at 11 years, 57 days.

The race for the batting title came down to the last game of the season. Brett entered play hitting .328 with Henderson hitting .325. Palmeiro entered hitting .319, but a late slide had already put him out of contention. So it was essentially a two-man race between Brett and Henderson.

Just like in 1980, the Royals crunched the numbers and figured out a way for Brett to win the batting title. The Royals thought Brett already was a first-ballot Hall of Famer, but if he became the first player to win batting crowns in three different decades, he would no doubt get into Cooperstown.

So to do this, the Royals chose not to start him. Brett later came on as a pinch-hitter and got a sacrifice fly and later singled. Henderson, meanwhile, went 1-for-3 and finished with a .325 average. Brett went 1-for-2 and finished hitting .329 to take the title. He also led the league with 45 doubles.

"It was just one of those things where it brought back memories of seeing the ball good and being patient, not trying to do too much with it, just trying to hit the ball hard somewhere, and I was able to do that the second half of the season," Brett said. "I don't know why I couldn't do it the first half, but the second half of the season I was able to do that."

Brett recorded his 3,000th hit in 1992 and retired in 1993, finishing his career with 317 homers, 3,154 hits, 1,596 RBIs, and a career batting average of .305. In Brett's final at-bat at Texas, he singled.

"I'll never forget his last game in Arlington," Art Stewart said. "Before the game, the writers all got around him and asked, 'George, what do you want to do your last time up to bat?' And everybody was wanting grand slam or home run or base hit to win the game. And he said, 'I want to hit the ball back to the pitcher and run like hell to first base.' And that typifies George Brett and the way he played the game. But you saw that as a young kid, and that's the one thing that I'll never forget about him."

Another No-Hitter

In recent years, the no-hitter has made a comeback across baseball. In some ways this can be considered good, and in some ways maybe not, which makes what

Part Three

Bret Saberhagen was the 1985 World Series MVP and won the Cy Young Award in 1985 and 1989. Saberhagen also threw the last Royals no-hitter in 1991. (Courtesy *Topeka Capital-Journal*)

happened on August 26, 1991, at Kauffman Stadium even more special for Royals fans.

On that night, the Royals were playing the Chicago White Sox, and Bret Saberhagen was on the mound. As he warmed up in the bullpen, Saberhagen felt super strong. Nine innings later, he threw the first and only no-hitter of his MLB career.

"Brent Mayne called a great game for me, and I kind of had everything going for me that night," Saberhagen said.

In the ninth, Saberhagen breezed through the top of the White Sox order, finishing it by retiring slugger Frank Thomas on a grounder to second, capping a 7-0 win. As smooth as that inning went, the no-hitter wasn't without controversy. For a minute, there was actually a White Sox hit on the scoreboard.

With one out in the fifth, Chicago's Dan Pasqua hit a liner toward the gap in left-center field. Left fielder Kirk Gibson gave chase, but as he reached the warning track, it appeared he lost sight of the ball. In an attempt to catch it, he sort of jumped and stabbed at the ball all in one motion.

The ball bounced off Gibson's glove, and Pasqua reached second base. Initially the play was ruled a double, but after viewing several replays, the official scorer changed it to a two-base error on Gibson, and the no-hitter remained intact.

Saberhagen, a native of Los Angeles, also threw a no-hitter in high school, pitching one as a senior for Reseda's Cleveland High in the City Section championship game in 1982 at Dodgers Stadium. Saberhagen's no-hitter was a bit of a surprise to the other scouts in attendance, but the Royals had considered Saberhagen a well-kept secret.

Like most teams, they initially viewed him as a shortstop, partly because he had lost some velocity due to a shoulder injury, as his fastball at one point was topping out in the high 70s. But the Royals changed their minds when Guy Hansen, who was a scout on the West Coast and later became a Royals pitching coach, attended one of Saberhagen's games his senior year. Hansen could see that Saberhagen's fastball was back into the high 80s, and he believed the pitcher had potential.

Art Stewart, a longtime scout, recalled the events of Saberhagen becoming a Royal like this:

"He was a pretty good athlete," Stewart said of Saberhagen. "He could play short pretty good. But this one day, Guy is out there to see him, and the pitcher gets knocked out, and they bring Saberhagen in, and he pitched like hell. And Guy sends the report in right away and says, 'This guy can pitch!' So based on that we took him in the nineteenth round, and then they were playing the state championship in LA at Dodgers Stadium, tons of scouts, and all the LA guys.

"The draft was over, but we had to wait to sign them until after that game was over. He goes out and pitches a no-hit shutout. The Dodger people, they were balling their scouts out and everybody for not knowing it."

For Saberhagen, his no-hitter with the Royals was no doubt a triumph. He went on the disabled list in mid-June and was out a month with inflammation in his rotator cuff, and the year before he had surgery to remove bone chips in his elbow. In those two years, Saberhagen went a combined 18-17 in 56 starts.

Saberhagen had a long history of pitching well in odd years and being injured in even years, and there were plenty of questions and concerns whether his arm would hold up in the future. But the no-hitter showed—at least for a day—that he was finally healthy and back in top form.

In the end, the no-hitter helped convince a team that he could still be a top starter long term. That team just wasn't the Royals.

So Long, Sabes

Pitchers usually control their own fate. It's what they want more than anything. On the mound, they've got the ball in hand, and it's up to them where it goes next.

Bret Saberhagen had control as good as any pitcher in the game when he played. His fastball popped gloves in the mid-'90s, and he could spot his breaking ball on the corner with ease. But the best pitcher in Royals history couldn't control what was going on behind the scenes.

The night of December 11, 1991, was seemingly going to be routine for Saberhagen. He was in his Southern California home with his family when the phone rang. Royals general manager Herk Robinson was on the other end. Robinson soon broke the news that Saberhagen had been traded to the New York Mets.

"I never thought I was going to leave," said Saberhagen, who went 110-78 with a 3.21 ERA in eight seasons in Kansas City.

In a blockbuster five-player deal, the Royals traded Saberhagen and infielder Bill Pecota to the Mets for Gregg Jeffries, Keith Miller, and Kevin McReynolds, all of whom were supposed to be starters for the Royals for the upcoming 1992 season.

During the winter meetings in Miami, the Mets were searching for a top starter to join a rotation that already had Dwight Gooden, David Cone, and Sid Fernandez. The Royals, meanwhile, were searching for a way to climb up the AL West standings after two consecutive next-to-last-place finishes, and parting with Saberhagen, the 1985 and 1989 Cy Young Award winner, was somehow supposed to help accomplish that.

After his conversation with Robinson ended, Saberhagen talked to George Brett. They recounted stories from the team's glory days and pondered the future without Saberhagen in Royal blue and how strange that would be. Saberhagen also called longtime friend and teammate Mark Gubicza.

"For the most part, the everyday players, they never moved," Gubicza said. "Mr. Kauffman was outstanding as far as keeping that core group together, and when he was traded it was kind of a shock. I was like, 'Nah, this ain't happening.'"

When the trade was announced, Royals fans were still smarting over trading Cone to the Mets, but the Saberhagen trade was a different type of furor. Because Saberhagen was so beloved, it hurt worse. Way worse.

To Royals fans, Saberhagen wasn't just the 1985 World Series MVP and a two-time Cy Young winner. He was Sabes, the curly-haired boy who grew up before their eyes but was now going far away to the East Coast and to the NL.

Saberhagen was just twenty-seven at the time. He had gone 13-8 with a 3.08 ERA that season and had just completed the first year of a three-year deal worth $8.9 million. In fact, Saberhagen's deal was the most lucrative in the history of the game when he signed it until Minnesota's Kirby Puckett became the first $3 million-a-year player a few days later.

Like the Cone trade, the Saberhagen trade didn't pan out for the Royals. All three acquisitions did little in a Royals uniform. Perhaps it was just a coincidence, but the Royals started the 1992 season 3-19 without Saberhagen. And they finished second to last in the division with a 72-90 record.

Saberhagen, as he did throughout his career, battled injuries in 1992 and appeared in just 17 games, going 3-5. The Mets also went 72-90 and finished next to last in the NL East. In 1995, the Mets traded Saberhagen to Colorado for the stretch run, and he pitched in one postseason game with the Rockies. Saberhagen sat out the 1996 season with a shoulder injury and signed with Boston that off-season. He continued to battle injuries with the Red Sox and finished his career in 2001. In the 10 years following the trade, Saberhagen won a combined 57 games.

Saberhagen was inducted into the Royals Hall of Fame in 2005. Today, Saberhagen lives in his native LA and stays busy running his charity—the Bret Saberhagen Make a Difference Foundation.

Saberhagen makes it back to Kansas City about three or four times a year, and in the summer of 2016, he participated in a celebrity softball game at Kauffman Stadium, where he was the starting pitcher, throwing on the same mound where he famously hugged Brett and earned a special place in Royals history.

"Looking back, I still enjoyed the other places I played," Saberhagen said. "I got to experience different fans, and different parts of the country, but my heart is still pretty much Kansas City."

The King Is Gone

When kings die, the immediate heir to the throne usually takes their place. But when Ewing Kauffman died on August 1, 1993, there was no one who could fill that void.

Kauffman, who had been suffering from bone cancer, died in his sleep at his home in Mission Hills, Kansas. He was seventy-six. The cancer was in a vertebra, and he had been in pain for months. When Kauffman's death was announced at Royals Stadium, flags were lowered to half-mast, and a moment of silence was observed as a city and Royals fans everywhere mourned.

Kansas City Royals founder Ewing Kauffman signs autographs for kids during a Royals game at old Municipal Stadium. Kauffman loved children so much that before his death he paid millions out of his own pocket to help put kids in the Kansas City area through college. (Courtesy *Ewing Marion Kauffman Foundation*)

Kauffman's last public appearance at Royals Stadium was May 21, 1993, when he was inducted into the Royals Hall of Fame. And in true Kauffman fashion, it was memorable. Dressed in a blue suit and Royals necktie, Kauffman smiled and began his speech.

"Ladies and gentlemen, you are well aware that the associates of the Royals earned all the awards that I have ever received," Kauffman told the crowd. "I'd also like to say without your support, and the Royal Lancers, we wouldn't have kept a baseball team in Kansas City.

"I ask you two questions: Will you write to your congressman and senator to keep Major League Baseball in Kansas City? Second question: How did you like your fighting Kansas City Royals?"

And with that, Kauffman walked away with a big smile, and to applause, as he and Muriel got in a Cadillac and were driven around the warning track, with Kauffman rolling down his window and giving the crowd one last wave.

Five years earlier, Kauffman, a man known for his generosity who also believed education was the key to success, started Project Choice. Kauffman told eighth-graders at Westport Middle School that he would pay their way through the college of their choice as long as they agreed to stay out of trouble, avoid teenage pregnancy, and graduate from high school.

Kauffman later expanded the program to other schools in the Kansas City area. In 2003, the Ewing Marion Kauffman Foundation launched the Kauffman Scholars program, which provides assistance to low-income students starting in the seventh grade and works with them until they graduate from college.

On what would have been his 100th birthday, the Kauffman Foundation announced a $79 million donation to the KC Scholars program, another new scholarship fund for low-income students, once again ensuring that Kauffman's legacy is far greater than a baseball team.

But owning the Royals was something his daughter Julia Irene Kauffman said he enjoyed "immensely." And with his health declining, Kauffman was unable to attend a ceremony in July 1993 when Royals Stadium was renamed Kauffman Stadium in his honor.

When she was a young girl, Julia would play card games with her father, but she insists she never won. And Kauffman, even near death, was still competitive, and innovative as ever. After no one stepped up to the plate to buy the team, Kauffman formulated a succession plan to keep the team in Kansas City after he died, donating nearly $100 million to keep the Royals afloat after his death.

In a final noble gesture, Kauffman gave the Royals to the Greater Kansas City Community Foundation with two conditions: the foundation would sell the team to someone who would keep it in Kansas City, and the proceeds from the sale would go to local charities. But the team went without an owner for seven years and was run by a board of directors during that time, and that's not exactly a recipe for success or stability.

Part Three

At Kauffman's funeral, the ceremony began with the playing of *The Star-Span-gled Banner*. He was buried in his Royals blue suit wearing his Royals tie and had an autographed baseball from the players in his hands. He also was buried with a bottle of whiskey and a deck of playing cards.

When his casket was removed from the church, the organist played *Take Me Out to the Ballgame*. And with Kauffman gone, it certainly was a different ballgame for his beloved Royals.

8

Foul Ball

Striking a Nerve

Ewing Kauffman didn't believe in unions. He figured if employers took care of their employees, there would be no need for them. The MLB Players Association, however, didn't share Kauffman's view on the matter.

On August 12, 1994, the players went on strike, initiating what became the longest work stoppage in baseball history. The strike lasted 232 days. More than 900 games were wiped out, including the 1994 postseason and World Series.

At the center of the conflict were the usual disagreements between the owners and players. Ever since the players were granted free agency in December 1975, owners have tried to curtail the rising cost of player salaries. After the owners were found guilty of colluding from 1985 to 1987, player salaries began to rise, and the gap between small-market and large-market teams began to widen.

Long before his death, Kauffman warned of the inequities of large-market vs. small-market baseball, and his franchise saw the ill effects of the disparity more than any other team. In the summer of 1994, most of the owners were in agreement that revenue sharing was imperative in order for the small-market teams to survive.

There were a few dissenters, mainly large-market owners. Still, led by acting Commissioner Bud Selig, who also owned the small-market Brewers at the time, the owners were intent on implementing revenue sharing and a salary cap. Selig said several teams were on the verge of financial collapse, and a salary cap was a must.

The Players Association and Union Chief Donald Fehr weren't going to stand for this, and subsequently neither side gave an inch. The Collective Bargaining Agreement of 1990 was set to expire on December 31, 1994, and the players set the strike date of August 12, believing the owners would blink first. Seven times before, there had been labor strikes in baseball, and all seven times the owners caved. But this time, the owners didn't, as they were largely unified in an attempt to control the rising cost of doing business.

Also at the forefront was Royals pitcher David Cone, who served as player rep for the AL. Cone, who was dealt to the Mets in spring training of 1987, had just returned to the Royals the year before, after Kauffman reeled in the Kansas City native during free agency.

"It just felt right to come back home," Cone said. "And it was really Ewing Kauffman, the late owner, who talked me into it. He sold me. He was a great salesman, and he was dying of bone cancer, and he made it clear to me that he thought the trade was the worst trade they ever made and he wanted to make it up.

"He made an unbelievably generous offer and structured the offer in a tremendous way for my benefit. He was a hard guy to say no to."

Cone's deal was for three years and $18 million and included a $9 million signing bonus—the largest in MLB history at the time. And it was paid up front. Money well spent in the eyes of Kauffman.

But for most of his tenure as owner, Kauffman wasn't big on big contracts. He spent big only when he absolutely had to. He paid George Brett and Bret Saberhagen well, and a few others. But in his late years, the Royals spent freely and unwisely on free agents. They even had the highest payroll in baseball in 1990 at $22 million in an effort to bring one more World Series championship to Kansas City before Kauffman died.

So put yourself in Cone's shoes. He had just signed a contract that at the time made him the game's highest-paid pitcher for one of baseball's smallest markets.

"It was a really tough time," Cone said. "That was the worst labor dispute in the history of the game, the World Series was canceled. There was a lot of animosity, and the Royals being a small-market team, and with Ewing Kauffman having passed away, it became a different organization at that point once he was gone. And I was a player rep, and there are a lot of variables involved with that.

"It was the most difficult thing I've ever been through, being a part of that at the time and on the frontlines. I was a representative, and it was exhausting, it was heartbreaking."

On August 12, 1994, the red-hot Royals were 64-51 and in third place in the AL Central, a game back of second-place Cleveland and just four behind the first-place White Sox. But they never got the chance to catch them. On September 14, the rest of the season and playoffs were canceled.

"It was difficult to deal with," Mark Gubicza said. "We were a pretty good team. We felt that even though Cleveland was a really, really good team, and Chicago, too, we felt that with our pitching it wouldn't matter.

"You win with pitching and defense, and we certainly had that. And when push comes to shove in the postseason, you never know what's going to happen or how it's going to turn out. But we thought that team had a shot and to never have that opportunity was pretty tough."

The day after baseball swallowed its season whole, the Royals fired manager Hal McRae. Without Kauffman around to pay the bills, the Royals soon became one of the game's most financially strapped franchises, and a youth movement began.

In October, the Royals hired Bob Boone to replace McRae, and later that month, the thirty-one-year-old Cone won the AL Cy Young Award with a 16-5 record and a 2.94 ERA. But Cone admitted there's something different about that particular award.

"There's always kind of an asterisk attached to that Cy Young," said Cone, who later donated the award to the Royals Hall of Fame.

As the 1994 calendar turned to December, the owners reached an impasse in negotiations with the MLBPA eight days before the collective bargaining agreement was set to expire and implemented a salary cap. In January 1995, owners declared they would use replacement players. Both times, the MLBPA filed a complaint with the National Labor Relations Board.

While Congress took a swing at MLB's antitrust exemption, the NLRB found that the owners' implementing the salary cap was illegal, and it was revoked on February 1, 1995. A few days later, President Bill Clinton met with Cone and other members of the MLBPA at the White House in hopes of reaching an agreement, but that did not happen. Later, Cone and others went before Congress on behalf of the players union.

In March, replacement players crossed the picket line and took the field for spring training games. Some teams, however, did not. The Orioles were one of the teams that didn't, and it made sense, as Cal Ripken was chasing Lou Gehrig's consecutive games played streak.

Without big leaguers in camp, there wasn't much excitement from fans during a time when hope was supposed to be eternal for every MLB team, including the Royals. Instead, there was really just a whole lot of anger, confusion, and resentment during what was one of the lowest points in professional sports history.

On April 2, 1995, the day before the regular season was set to begin, a federal judge issued an injunction against the owners, and baseball would resume with a 144-game regular-season schedule under the conditions of the expired CBA. This meant the Royals were still not on solid financial ground.

On a $40.5 million payroll, the Royals lost about $16 million in 1994. In 1995, the Royals wanted to keep their payroll at about $30 million, and that meant they had to shed $9 million in salary, so expensive veterans were quickly dealt. On April 5, center fielder Brian McRae, who made $1.9 million in 1994 and was set to receive a hefty pay raise through arbitration, was dealt to the Cubs.

"This team went from being a contending team in '93 and '94 to a joke for almost another decade," McRae said. "That was tough. Even though I was playing somewhere else that was tough because I have been associated with this organization since 1973, and from the time I was associated with this organization with my dad getting traded here and growing up and watching them and then being drafted by the ballclub, the team won for the most part."

The day after McRae was traded, the Royals traded Cone to Toronto. When Cone reported to Royals camp, he immediately knew something was up. He could see it in Boone's eyes.

"When I showed up he gave me a funny look like, 'What are you doing here?'" Cone said. "And people were scrambling around that first day, and I could tell something was up. So the next day, the trade came down and I was sent to Toronto. So I wasn't really surprised at that point. That was such a tough time after the strike."

After three weeks of spring training, baseball returned on April 25, 1995. But more damage would be done, with the Royals eventually shedding more payroll and departing with more veterans.

"You heard rumblings of small market versus large market," Gubicza said. "But the way Mr. K ran this club we always thought we were a large-market team playing in a smaller city. All of the sudden we knew all of those veterans were going to be gone, and basically at that point I'm the lone survivor of the World Series team, and the lone survivor as far as anyone having any length of time here with the club."

In 1997, baseball implemented revenue sharing and a luxury tax on payrolls, but that did little to help the Royals' struggles. The 2002 CBA tweaked the framework of the luxury tax—which was $117 million in 2003 and $189 million in 2016—to be a little more generous to small-market teams. And combined with new revenue streams from stadium upgrades and TV packages, baseball is much healthier today, making the likelihood of another strike like the one in 1994 unlikely.

"Everybody was tested on both sides, both labor and management," Cone said. "Everyone was tested to their limits, and I hope we never see that again. I don't think we will."

Quiz Saves Best for Last

On May 30, 1998, Dan Quisenberry was inducted into the Royals Hall of Fame. In the midst of another losing season, bringing back part of the team's past for one last outing provided relief that was—in true Quisenberry fashion—wonderful.

But what Quisenberry was going through at the time was anything but. In December 1997, he was diagnosed with a Stage IV malignant brain tumor. The following month, he underwent surgery, and 80 to 90 percent of the tumor was removed. But Stage IV is often the endgame.

With his health declining, there was some concern Quiz wouldn't be able to make it through the special night at Kauffman Stadium. But Quisenberry, the friendly jokester and submariner who played for the Royals from 1979 to 1988 and often hosed down the fans in right field, delighted the crowd of 30,341 once again with his grace and humor.

"I'm so blessed. I've got this great family," an emotional Quisenberry said before he embraced his wife, Janie, son, David, and daughter, Alysia, in a group hug. "And I played in a special time in this city for the Kansas City Royals. I loved playing in those years with those guys in this stadium in front of you folks, great fans, great city and a great team.

"This is more than I deserve. This is great. God bless you all, and thanks for the prayers. Thank you very much."

A dry eye could not be found in the stadium.

"That was a hard year for us," Janie recalled. "It's something he always wanted. He always wanted to be in the Royals Hall of Fame. It was a special night, but it also was a hard night.

Part Three

Also known for his smile and great sense of humor, Dan Quisenberry (left) was loved by every-one, especially teammates, including catcher Jim Sundberg. (Courtesy *Topeka Capital-Journal*)

"A brain tumor is a hard thing to have, and you're really weary and tired, and you kind of want to be on for everybody. And it was great to have family in the stands, but it also was very exhausting for him, and it was a very emotional night for our family."

Dan and Janie met at La Verne University in California. She was studying to be a teacher, and she and Dan had Bible study and dance class together. The baseball players were in the class because the coach believed it would help their agility.

Janie wasn't that into baseball as a young girl. She would occasionally go see the Dodgers' minor league team in Bakersfield with her grandfather, but when she met Dan, baseball became a big part of her life.

"One of the funniest things was when I went to visit him in the minor leagues in Waterloo, Iowa, and he taught me how to keep score so I would understand the game," Janie said. "And after the game we'd go through how I kept score, and he'd explain different things and stuff, so I learned that way.

"And one of the games as a relief pitcher, he pitched about nine innings. It was a doubleheader that lasted I think nineteen innings that first game, and he pitched nine innings and didn't give up a hit. He didn't give up a run, but we didn't score a run either."

Long outings were often the norm for Quisenberry, who was undrafted but pitched more than 100 innings five times as the Royals closer. One of his favorite memories was when he set what was then the MLB single-season saves record with 45 in 1983.

"That was a big deal for him," Janie said. "He wasn't a big name, and they didn't ever really expect that he was going to get here or that he would be so successful."

Quisenberry would often do crossword puzzles and word games in the bullpen, and after he retired in 1990, he became a poet later in life. His book *On Days Like This: Poems* was released in 1998.

"He would like to play with words," Janie said. "Denny Matthews and he would always have this game of a word here and a word there and trying to use that word in an interview. And he was good. He enjoyed writing and poetry. He'd write some poems about baseball and some would be about our kids. Some would be true stories and some were observations of people and some would be his creative mind."

A month after his Hall of Fame ceremony, Quisenberry had another surgery when the cancer had spread. But doctors were unable to remove all of the tumor. Quisenberry died on September 30, 1998, at age forty-five.

Quisenberry certainly left his mark on the Royals. His 2.55 ERA is the best in team history, and he is second in saves (238), trailing only Jeff Montgomery (304). Quisenberry was a three-time All-Star (1982–84) and led the AL in saves five times and was the Fireman of the Year five times. But Quisenberry might best be remembered for his smile and how he made everyone feel.

"He was very beloved," Janie said. "He had a great sense of humor. He was very genuine, he was very real. He was caring, he'd love to talk with you and ask questions. He loved the Lord and faith was a big part of his life. He was a really good man and he was funny, but everybody knows that. He had a very caring heart and was a deep thinker."

The Glass Ceiling

Before his death, Ewing Kauffman handpicked David Glass to be his successor as owner of the Royals. Kauffman's endorsement, however, did little to sway fans into Glass's corner.

Glass grew up in Mountain View, Missouri, and graduated from Missouri State with a business degree. He made a name in the business world serving as president and CEO of Walmart, helping lead the company to unprecedented growth. Following Kauffman's death, Glass was appointed the team's chairman of the board, essentially making him the team's unofficial owner.

In some ways, Glass and Kauffman had similar ideals. Glass was a firm believer in a salary cap, and in 1996 he voted against baseball's CBA. But the transition after Kauffman's death was rough. Low payrolls, youth movements, and a whole lot of losing were all common themes for years. Glass was initially considered a favorite to purchase the team after Kauffman died, but he eventually backed out when he thought Kansas City would not support his bid. That opened the doors for Miles Prentice, a lawyer from New York.

For a time, Prentice, Lamar Hunt, and George Brett were all in the bidding to own the Royals. But Hunt and Brett's offer was below the set minimum price of $75 million. Prentice's bid, however, was for $75 million, and the Royals approved his bid in 1998.

Prentice's bid was a large one—not so much in terms of dollars, but in terms of people. His group at one point had about forty investors, and MLB rejected his bid in November 1999, putting the Royals back at square one. Soon after Prentice's bid failed, Glass was back in the picture.

"I feel that this is the right time for me to step forward and try and fulfill the promise I made to Ewing Kauffman," Glass said in a statement announcing his plans to buy the team.

On April 17, 2000, MLB approved Glass's $96 million bid for the Royals, formally beginning a somewhat tumultuous relationship between Glass and the fans—one that would take years to repair.

Showing Some Fight

Mike Sweeney is known to give more hugs than handshakes, and more smiles and encouraging words than frowns. He is a devout Catholic and would say a prayer before he stepped onto the diamond. But there is another side to Sweeney: his fighting side. And that was on full display the night of August 10, 2001.

The Royals were playing the Detroit Tigers at Kauffman Stadium, and Sweeney came up to bat in the bottom of the sixth inning against Jeff Weaver. The Royals were 25 games under .500 and were trailing 2-1 on the scoreboard.

Carlos Beltran had just doubled to right field, and Sweeney was up next. The Royals would lose 97 games that season, which at the time was a tie for the most in franchise history. The Royals also were seemingly breaking apart as a franchise. Johnny Damon, Jermaine Dye, and Rey Sanchez, who were close friends of Sweeney, had all been traded away for nothing in cost-cutting moves, and another lost season was crashing down.

Damon had been dealt before the season to Oakland in exchange for an old closer named Roberto Hernandez, backup catcher A.J. Hinch, and shortstop Angel Berroa, the prized prospect in the deal. Dye and Sanchez were both shipped out before the trade deadline, with Dye going to Oakland via the Colorado Rockies for shortstop Neifi Perez and Sanchez to the Braves for oh, who cares? So the biggest thing to watch down the stretch of that miserably horrible season was to see if the Royals actually would lose 100 games for the first time in history.

But as Weaver stood on the mound, Sweeney was bothered not so much by the trades themselves but by something else: the rosin bag.

The rosin bag normally is placed behind the mound at the back of the dirt, but on this occasion, it was too close to the pitching rubber and was distracting Kansas City's slugger. So Sweeney asked the home plate umpire to have Weaver move it back. Weaver scoffed, and as the umpire walked back to home plate, Weaver challenged Sweeney's manhood, sending a couple of F-bombs his way before turning his back to Sweeney.

No matter how strong and how disciplined, every man has his breaking point. And this was Sweeney's. He dropped the bat. The umpire tried to stop him by corralling him in his arms. But Sweeney wouldn't be stopped. He sidestepped his way free and charged the mound. Weaver—with his back turned—was unaware that there was an enraged 6-foot-3, 225-pound man heading his way.

"Jeremy Affeldt had a great quote one time," Sweeney said. "He said, 'You know what? Mike Sweeney's a big teddy bear, but if you cross the line, that teddy bear becomes a grizzly bear.' I always prided myself on being a great teammate, playing the game hard every single night. But my teammates always knew that if there was ever a line that you crossed with me, and when you do, I have that grizzly bear side in me.

Mike Sweeney follows through on his game-winning single that delivered the Royals a 5-4 win over Boston in 2006. Sweeney played thirteen seasons in Kansas City and was a five-time All-Star. (Courtesy *REUTERS/Dave Kaup*)

"That's what fueled me to be the player I was. I never settled for mediocrity, I always strived for greatness. And that night with Jeff Weaver, I don't regret it because I felt that was the thing to do, to stick up for my teammates and for the Royals organization. We played together, we fought together, we lost together, we cried together. That's what brothers do, that's what teammates do."

As the crowd roared, Weaver turned around to see Sweeney barreling down on him with his helmet in hand. The helmet hit Weaver in the arm, and moments later, after a few jabs, Sweeney drove Weaver to the ground. Sweeney got in a few more shots before a teammate pulled him away from the mass of bodies that engulfed the infield. But the fight didn't end there.

Round two began moments after Sweeney went to pick up his helmet. Near home plate, Detroit catcher Robert Fick took a swing, narrowly missing Sweeney's face. Sweeney's teammate Paul Byrd then swooped in and hogtied Fick on the ground, giving Sweeney an opening to get a few more punches in before he hit the showers.

Sweeney was held out of the lineup the next night because he jammed his wrist in the melee. He sat out five games with his injured wrist and then was suspended 10 games for his role in the brawl. Sweeney thought about appealing his suspension, but his wrist was swollen enough that he would have missed several games anyway, so he chose not to fight it.

Sweeney's career with the Royals was actually an underdog fight from the start. He was drafted as a catcher in the tenth round of the 1991 draft and made it to the big leagues in September 1995. Sweeney struggled early in his career, and in 1999, he began the season as the team's third-string catcher, and because of a rash of injuries he was also being used as the team's designated hitter at times. But after veteran first baseman Jeff King retired in May, the Royals needed a first baseman fast.

"I was one of Jeff King's best friends on the team," Sweeney said. "And I was the one who was trying to talk him out of retiring."

King, though, wouldn't budge. Injuries had taken their toll, but King's young son was a special needs child, and his family needed him back home at their Wyoming ranch. So King walked away from a two-year contract, forgoing about $3 million. After King retired, Sweeney eventually nailed down the job at first base, hitting .322 with 22 homers and 102 RBIs in 1999. And the rest is history. But in Sweeney's case, once again it almost wasn't.

On an off day in 1999, Sweeney and teammates Jed Hansen and Jeremy Giambi went fishing on Kevin Appier's exotic farm in Paola, Kansas. The farm featured llamas, camels, and other furry things. After they caught some bass, it was time to catch the team bus and get to the airport. But first, Giambi went for a spin on Appier's Honda Odyssey.

Giambi used to race ATVs as a kid, and he climbed inside the four-wheeler, ducking his head beneath the roll cage to get in. Giambi took off, tearing through a cornfield. The first time, Giambi walked away unscathed. But the second time, he wasn't so lucky.

Not wearing a helmet, he took a jump too fast and hit his head on the top of the cage and rolled the vehicle three times before it landed on its wheels. When Giambi got out, he was bleeding from head to toe.

Rushed to the hospital, Giambi had to get staples in his head to stop the blood. The ballplayers barely made the team flight, but Giambi, who was supposed to platoon with Sweeney at first, was unable to play the next day, and Sweeney became the team's everyday first baseman.

Sweeney hit 197 home runs with 838 RBIs and had a .299 career average in thirteen seasons with the Royals. Not bad for someone who was told he had "no chance" to make the team out of spring training in 1999.

"I never dreamt that when Jeff King retired it would open up a door for me to cross in my career," said Sweeney, who was inducted into the Royals Hall of Fame in 2015. "Had he not retired, I may have got released and ended up going back to Southern California to bag groceries."

In 2000, when the Royals were setting offensive records, Sweeney played in the first of five All-Star Games and set a franchise record for RBIs in a season with 144. In 2002, he hit .340, second in the league to Manny Ramirez. But one of Sweeney's greatest honors of his career was when George Brett gave him his jersey with a C on it before Opening Day in 2003.

"George Brett came in and he gave me my jersey, and I sat there with tears in my eyes as my teammates gave me a standing ovation in the locker room," said Sweeney, who served as the team's captain until 2007. "I'll never forget that moment as long as I live. George Brett has become one of my good friends, and to receive that honor was incredible."

Sweeney's career with the Royals ended in 2007, and though it's not technically retired, no one has worn No. 29 since. In 2008, the Royals created the Mike Sweeney Award, an award given to a player who best represents the organization on and off the field. That's obviously a pretty high standard, even more so when you consider that Sweeney has turned down offers to be an MLB hitting coach the last few years so he could remain in the Royals front office.

Sweeney, like Brett, played with heart, passion, and fire. And that August night in 2001 was the only time Sweeney was ever ejected from a game. Sweeney and Weaver have since made peace, but it took time. They did not talk for five years following the incident until one day, shortly before Christmas, Sweeney called Weaver and asked for forgiveness.

Weaver was receptive to Sweeney's wish, and the two wished their families well. But Sweeney is a man of conviction. And just like he did that night he charged the mound, he still bleeds Royal blue. And he always will.

"I've spoken with Jeff Weaver, and we've cleared the air and we've put that in the past, so we're good there," Sweeney said. "I don't hold any resentment or bitterness toward him. That's something that happened, and looking back if it happened 100 times, 100 times the same result would probably happen, but I certainly don't regret it."

A Royal Flush

Scott Boras has caused many general managers across baseball to lose sleep at night. And dating back to the 1990s, no agent in the game evokes feelings of anger, fear, and loathing to Royals fans more than Boras.

Boras, meanwhile, generally speaking, hates two things: small-market teams and signing contract extensions before free agency. It's a strategy that over the years has worked well for Boras and his clients, who are typically the most sought-after players during the winter.

Some of these top Boras clients have worn the Royals uniform. But by the time they hit free agency they were no longer in Kansas City because the Royals were forced to get whatever they could for their star players in trades that were laughable and unbearable to stomach, and that applied to the Carlos Beltran trade.

On June 24, 2004, the Royals in a three-team deal shipped Beltran—a Boras client—to Houston and received third baseman Mark Teahen, catcher John Buck, and right-hander Mike Wood from Oakland. The trade marked the final gut punch to Royals fans who enjoyed watching the best outfield in baseball in 1999 and 2000 with Beltran in center field, Jermaine Dye in right, and Johnny Damon—a Boras client—in left.

Beltran and his wife were at Mike Sweeney's new home for a barbecue the evening of the trade. Sweeney and his wife were nearly finished giving a tour when Beltran's phone rang and he learned of the news. Just hours before, the Royals played Detroit in a day game, and Beltran and Sweeney homered in what would be one of 104 losses that season.

The trade—like Damon's and Dye's—was a result of a lot of losing and not enough money to keep the star player. But as bad as the Royals' financial situation was at the time, here's a twist: the Royals could have re-signed Beltran. They really could have, if only they had a million dollars more to close the deal.

Beltran actually went behind Boras's back and negotiated a below-market deal with the Royals. At one point, the Royals offered Beltran $23 million for three years. But Boras wanted $24 million for his superstar client who would hit free agency after the 2004 season, so no new contract was completed.

Beltran was selected to the AL All-Star team, but because of the trade he was awarded a spot on the NL squad as an Astro. Beltran helped the Astros make the playoffs, and he signed a seven-year deal for $119 million with the Mets that offseason. Beltran then played with Giants, Cardinals, and Yankees before being traded to Texas at the trade deadline in 2016. Back in the AL, Beltran became a yearly visitor to Kauffman Stadium, but he never felt out of place.

"Growing up in this organization, this organization is always going to be in my heart, the Royals are," Beltran said on a return visit with the Yankees.

Teahen and Buck were starters and had a couple decent seasons—by Royals standards—but nothing major. And in 2005, the Royals lost a franchise record 106 games, sinking to a new level of darkness. But there would be light.

PART FOUR

A ROYAL REBIRTH

A lifelong Royals fan and Kansas native, Dayton Moore wasn't all smiles when he first took over as general manager for the Kansas City Royals in 2006. But since he's been in charge, the franchise has gone from being cellar dwellers to perennial playoff contenders. (Courtesy *USA TODAY Sports*/*Kirby Lee*)

9

Fixing the Mess

The Architect Arrives

Dayton Moore had it all planned out from the start. The Plaza is where the Royals would have the World Series parade.

A World Series parade in Kansas City!? That was an unbelievable notion when Moore was hired as Royals general manager on May 31, 2006. At the time, the Royals had the worst record in baseball at 13-38, and they had lost 100 games in three of the previous four seasons. So the Royals job wasn't exactly a good one. In fact, it was probably one of the worst jobs in the history of baseball.

For weeks prior to Moore's arrival, rumors swirled that Royals general manager Allard Baird was going to be let go. But when Braves GM John Schuerholz asked Moore, his top assistant and the hottest commodity in baseball, to have lunch with him in Atlanta, Moore figured they might just discuss the upcoming draft and it would be just another normal lunch. But it wasn't. Schuerholz told him the Royals were making a change at general manager.

For years, Moore didn't really have any interest in becoming a GM. He was quite content working under Schuerholz. But sentiment has a way of pulling one close to the past and believing it could again be the future. Moore grew up in Wichita and was a lifelong Royals fan, and as a kid he listened to Royals games on the radio with his grandmother in Coldwater, Kansas.

One night, Moore and his roommate were driving from Illinois to Garden City Community College in western Kansas, where Moore played baseball. That particular night was Game Seven of the 1985 World Series. Unable to afford tickets, they watched the game from across I-70. Back then, a chain-link fence was all that separated the freeway from the ballpark, so the view wasn't bad at all. Moore could see everything except left field.

So when Schuerholz told Moore that David and Dan Glass were coming to Atlanta and they wanted to speak with him, Moore knew immediately he would agree to an interview. A few days later, Moore met with them, and it was clear from the start what direction they wanted to go.

"I had never met him, but it was obvious that Mr. Glass wanted to build something special, and he wanted to do it the right way, and he was going to give us full support," Moore said. "And we knew this would be an unbelievable place from a fan perspective and an environment perspective if we could win, and we were also excited about the challenge."

The challenge for Moore was to rebuild from the organization from the bottom up through the draft, player development, and trades. He also had to change the losing culture of the franchise so it could win by 2013. Getting more talent in the system was one thing, but changing the culture was another. The following are just a few things that happened before Moore arrived.

In 2001 after a loss to Cleveland that dropped the Royals' record to 10-18, ex-Marine-turned-manager Tony Muser talked eloquently of milk and cookies. And tequila.

"Chewing on cookies and drinking milk and praying is not going to get it done," Muser said after the loss. "It's going to take a lot of hard work and some mindset. And I think there's a lot of transition going on in that room."

"I'd like to see them go out and pound tequila rather than cookies and milk because nobody's going to get us out of this but us," Muser added.

Muser later received a bottle of tequila in the mail from a fan. He kept it as a trophy—the only trophy the Royals ever got during his tenure. Muser was fired in April 2002 with a 317-431 record in parts of six seasons as Royals manager.

Muser was replaced by Tony Peña, who led the team to an 83-79 record in 2003 and was the AL Manager of the Year. The future sort of looked bright for 2004, but after he lost five in a row in mid-April, the tension was so palpable, Peña hit the showers. Literally! He actually took a shower with his uniform on to motivate his players.

"I had to do something," Peña said at the time. "Make them laugh. Well, they laughed."

In May 2005, the Royals were 8-25, and Peña quit one night after a game, ending his tenure with a record of 198-285. Peña was replaced by Buddy Bell, and the team lost 19 in a row late in the season. The following year, on April 19, 2006, the Royals lost 4-0 to the White Sox. It was their tenth straight defeat, and the team was 2-12 on the season. Here's how Bell described the state of the Royals franchise at the time.

"I never say it can't get worse," Bell said.

Between the white lines there also were some memorable miscues, and first baseman Ken Harvey—an All-Star in 2004—had a knack for being in the wrong place at the wrong time. He once got wedged between the tarp and the fence chasing a foul ball and was stuck there for several minutes. He also got hit in the back on a throw from the outfield that was headed to home plate and also had a nasty collision with relief pitcher Jason Grimsley when fielding a grounder to first and attempting to throw home.

Moore was told by many people across baseball that the Royals were a lost cause and that he couldn't win in Kansas City. At one point, he even told his wife, Marianne, that he would remain with the Braves before he changed his mind and accepted the Royals' job. His introductory press conference was hostile in the sense that most of the questions were to Glass regarding Baird's firing and not about Moore and the team's future.

To fix the Royals, Moore had some built-in advantages Baird did not. For starters, payroll climbed steadily. In 2006, the payroll was about $46 million, and in 2016, the Royals spent about $137 million.

Moore did not participate in the Royals' 2006 draft, as he officially began his duties June 8.

Moore's first draft as Royals GM thus came in 2007, and with the second overall pick, the Royals selected Mike Moustakas. In the third round, the Royals selected left-hander Danny Duffy, and in the tenth round they picked Greg Holland. And in 2008, the Royals picked Eric Hosmer third overall.

The Royals also expanded their efforts internationally and signed Salvador Perez (2006), Kelvin Herrera (2006), and Yordano Ventura (2008), eventually putting together the best farm system in baseball. Though there are a lot of moving parts to being a general manager, Moore's basic philosophy is not complicated.

"We stay focused on trying to get better each and every day," Moore said. "You can't attach yourself to the outcome because you just have to try to get better every single day. We've had great support from ownership and our entire staff. We've felt that we were constantly building in a way that's going to put us in a position to be successful so you just kept a strong, positive mindset."

That was extremely difficult at times. Bell stepped down following the 2007 season, and Moore hired Trey Hillman, who had success as a manager in the minors with the Yankees and was managing in Japan at the time of his hiring. The Royals went 75-87 his first season in 2008, then fell to 65-97 and finished in last place in 2009 despite having Cy Young Award winner Zack Greinke.

After a 12-23 start to 2010, Moore fired Hillman and replaced him with Ned Yost, with whom he had worked in Atlanta. The Royals lost 95 games that season but played better under Yost. Still, the losing took its toll, and Greinke demanded a trade. In December 2010, the Royals complied, sending him to Milwaukee for Lorenzo Cain and Alcides Escobar.

There was some backlash over the deal, but Moore and Yost, who had seen Cain and Escobar play when he was manager of the Brewers, believed they had acquired championship-caliber players. And Moore believed that the 2011 season was time to "flip the switch" on the process fans had been waiting years to see.

Salvy Makes a Splash

Dayton Moore still remembers the call. It was 2007, and Royals special assistant Bill Fischer was on the line. Fischer was watching a young catcher named Salvador Perez, who was just getting started in the Arizona Rookie League.

"I just saw the Venezuelan version of Johnny Bench," said Fischer, who once was pitching coach of the Big Red Machine.

Moore's ears perked with interest. He had known Fischer since his first year in pro ball in 1994, and Moore said Fischer "isn't somebody that hands out those types of comparisons or compliments." Naturally, Moore had to see Perez for himself—again. Moore first saw Perez when the team signed him at age sixteen.

"I remember the way he had such a vibrant personality, and that hasn't changed," Moore said. "I knew he could catch and throw."

In the minors, Perez flew somewhat under the radar, but the Royals had high hopes for him. The 2011 season is one Moore looks back on as a stepping-stone for the organization as his first wave of young talent arrived, joining Alex Gordon and Billy Butler in the big leagues. Eric Hosmer and Danny Duffy made their debuts that May, Mike Moustakas came along in June, and Perez made his debut August 10 at Tampa Bay. That night, Perez got his first big-league hit off Wade Davis, and he also drove in and scored in a run. But it was his play behind the plate that caught everyone's attention.

Since his arrival in Kansas City in 2011, Royals catcher Salvador Perez has made many Royals fans smile with his energy and enthusiasm as well as his famous "Salvy Splash" after a Royals' win. Here he is splashing Mike Moustakas in 2015. (Courtesy *USA TODAY Sports/Denny Medley*)

In the fourth, Perez showed off his arm by picking off a runner at first. In the eighth, he picked off a runner at third—the first pickoffs by a Royals catcher that season. The Rays didn't attempt to steal on Perez, who has been clocked as fast as 1.8 seconds on throws to second base. The league average is around. 2.0.

In his MLB debut, it was clear that Perez was a special ballplayer in another way, as he became an instant fan favorite with his smile, energy, and happiness on the diamond.

"It's my job, and I love it," Perez said. "I love to play the game."

"His happiness and his passion, his love for the game is authentic," Duffy said. "There's nothing artificial about it."

Perez also brought with him something that has since become a Royals tradition: the Salvy Splash. After a win, a smiling Perez can be found in the dugout near the Gatorade bucket. Perez said it's his job to "make it rain," so when the star of the game is doing a postgame interview on the field, Perez runs out with the water cooler and douses the player.

"I just decided to do it one day and I liked it," Perez said.

The Royals went 71-91 in 2011, and in the offseason they signed Perez, who had played in just 39 games, to a five-year contract worth $7 million. Perez, however, injured his knee in spring training and didn't play until June, and the Royals finished 72-90 in 2012.

Despite the record, Moore saw enough progress to believe the team could compete the next season if he acquired some pitching. In December 2012, Moore dipped into his stock of minor league talent and acquired James Shields and Davis from Tampa Bay for top prospect Wil Myers, Jake Odorizzi, and Mike Montgomery. The Royals were now ready to win—or so they thought.

By George, Brett's Back

The 2013 season was supposed to be the year the Royals took that big step forward. In the end, it was. But for a couple weeks in May, it looked like the biggest rebuilding projected in baseball history might crumble and fall.

In a desperate hour, general manager Dayton Moore believed the Royals needed to be "rescued." So he picked up the phone and called George Brett. Brett's wife, Leslie, was out of town, and he was at home with his two youngest sons, Dylan and Robin.

Brett had been offered a job as hitting coach a few times over the years by several organizations, including the Royals. But this time it was different for Brett. Still, he wouldn't quite say yes. So later, Royals manager Ned Yost called Brett.

After being retired for twenty years, George Brett was happy to put on a Royals uniform again when he served as the team's hitting coach for two months during the 2013 season. Here he is smiling during the seventh inning in a game against the Texas Rangers in Arlington, Texas. (Courtesy *REUTERS/Tim Sharp*)

"Let me think about it," Brett said.

The next night the Royals lost at St. Louis, their eighth consecutive defeat. How could this happen? James Shields was brought in to lead the rotation, and the team had a bunch of budding young stars seemingly ready to take that next step. But the Royals weren't hitting, and they were now in last place.

Being at the bottom certainly wasn't anything new for the Royals, but something bigger was at stake. The franchise's losing culture was threatening to envelop the new crop of prospects who were supposed to return it to glory.

Part Four

Brett wouldn't stand for this. He couldn't just sit there and do nothing as the franchise he loved so dearly was spiraling further into the abyss. He didn't know how good he would be at it, but he had to try.

"I was just real frustrated with the way they were swinging the bats," Brett said.

The following afternoon on May 30, Brett, who had just turned sixty two weeks before, was named the Royals interim hitting coach with Pedro Grifol serving as his assistant. Co-hitting coaches Jack Maloof and Andre David were reassigned.

Numbers aside, Brett's main goal as the Royals hitting coach was pretty straight-forward. He wanted the team to win. In Brett's first game back, the Royals beat the Cardinals 4-2. Because he was wearing his famous No. 5 again, fans had a reason to show up early and watch batting practice, as many were seeing Brett in uniform for the first time. For Brett, the return to life in the majors was quite an adjustment.

"It's still a little strange getting back into baseball," Brett said that June during a BP session at Kauffman Stadium. "I'm 20 years away. The game's changed an awful lot. There are indoor cages everywhere. We used to do all of our hitting on the field and now guys do it in the cages, they have routines and certain times they hit, and it's just kind of a different game."

Upon taking the job, there was one condition. Brett told Moore that he would stay on for a month and reevaluate after that. Brett didn't really want to leave his family and endure the 162-game grind. He had to do that late in his playing career and didn't like it. He also had "a pretty good life" as the team's vice president of baseball operations. He could travel, attend his kids' games, and play golf. But a month-long commitment didn't seem so bad.

During his introductory news conference in St. Louis announcing his return to the game, Brett spoke about Gerber baby food and getting rid of bottles, meaning it was time for these kids to grow up and produce. One of Brett's first tasks was fixing Eric Hosmer's swing. Brett wanted the first baseman to start his swing earlier, so he had him move his hands back toward his ear. It worked, as Hosmer started to pull the ball again and hit for power.

"He's a tremendous hitting guy," Hosmer said at the time. "And just having him in the dugout has been real beneficial for us, and seeing him around the cage and picking his brain has been awesome. Having a guy like George Brett—who is probably one of the top baseball players of all-time—with you is a pretty neat experience."

During that hot summer day at the park, Brett told me one of the teaching points he would share with young hitters. It went like this:

"Say five numbers, one to five, in any random order, slow," Brett said.

"Three, two, one, four, five," I responded.

"Now put up a different amount of fingers than you say," Brett said.

The trick was to see how many players (and me) would actually hold up one number and say a different number. For example, when done correctly, the player might hold up two fingers and say "Five!" Most players, however, couldn't do this more than three or four times in a row unless they had developed some sort of a pattern.

"See," Brett said. "Now if you're thinking about your fundamentals, how are you going to see a ball coming at you?"

Brett's point was this: Think about one thing at a time. And his philosophy on hitting is pretty simple: "See the ball, hit the ball." But doing that isn't so easy. So Brett preached to the players to work on fundamentals in practice and when the game starts, see the ball and hit it.

Brett learned the art of hitting from Charlie Lau, who was the team's longtime hitting coach in the '70s. Lau always stressed fundamentals and so did Brett, who also shared this bit of knowledge with me:

"When your fundamentals are good, and you don't have to think about them, you see the ball better. The better you see the ball, the harder you're going to hit it. The harder you hit it, the higher your average. The higher your average, the more money you make. The more money you make, the more your wife loves you. That's a little poem Charlie Lau and I came up with," Brett said with a laugh.

Brett stayed on as hitting coach for two months but left the job for a number of reasons.

"I quit the job because I didn't think I was getting through to a lot of them," Brett told me years later. "A lot of them weren't paying attention to what I was saying. And after playing baseball for twenty years and doing that travel schedule for twenty years, then not doing it for twenty years, and getting back into that schedule, I hated it. I was in a bad mood every day, and the one thing you can't do is go down to the dugout or in that locker room and be in a bad mood every day.

"The players, they got to be upbeat. And I was always bitching. I was always pissed off at something. I had a long talk with Dayton, I had a long talk with Pedro, and a lot of guys were spending time with him and not me. So I thought it was a perfect time to go."

On July 25, 2013, the day after the thirtieth anniversary of the Pine Tar Game, Brett returned to the front office, and Grifol was named the team's hitting coach. The next day, the Royals embarked on a ten-day, nine-game road trip. And for Brett, it was time to return home.

Statistically, the Royals were worse with Brett as hitting coach. They batted .261 before his arrival and were thirteenth in runs scored at 3.98 runs per game. After Brett came on board, they hit .248 and averaged 3.81 runs a game. But there was progress.

Hosmer and Mike Moustakas showed signs they could reach their full potential and lead Kansas City back to prominence. And, in the end, Brett helped the Royals achieve his main goal. During his tenure, the Royals went 26-22 and climbed from last to third in the AL Central standings.

"George is a huge influence on our entire front office and our entire baseball team and the entire organization," Moore said. "So anything that George Brett's a part of is successful in wins and that's been apparent from Day One."

The Royals finished 86-76 in 2013, their first winning season since the 2003 season. Though they missed out on the playoffs for the twenty-eighth straight year, it was a big step forward for the franchise, which was about to go on quite a run.

The Wild Card Game

On September 30, 2014, the Royals returned to the postseason for the first time in twenty-nine years. A few days earlier, the Royals defeated the White Sox 3-1 to clinch at least a wild-card berth. The Royals finished with 89 wins during the regular season—one game back of Detroit in the AL Central—so they got to host the wild-card game against Oakland.

At long last, the dreams of many became reality, and the night ended with Salvador Perez getting a walk-off hit down the third-base line that scored Christian Colon to give the Royals a thrilling 9-8 comeback win in twelve innings in a game that lasted 4 hours, 45 minutes.

"This is the best moment," Perez said inside a jubilant Royals clubhouse with beer and champagne spraying everywhere. "I feel great."

In the twelfth, the A's took an 8-7 lead on a single by Alberto Callaspo. But with winter just two outs away, the Royals rallied. Eric Hosmer walked to the plate, telling himself to battle and keep the line moving. Hosmer did just that, putting a jolt into the stadium as he tripled off the wall in left-center field. Colon, a backup infielder, came on to pinch-hit for speedster Terrance Gore, who earlier had run for Billy Butler.

Colon was looking to get something in the air to score Hosmer, and he did, hitting a high chopper off the plate. A's third baseman Josh Donaldson had no chance to get Hosmer, who slid home safely and celebrated with a yell and a left-handed punch that would have knocked somebody out.

Kansas City Royals catcher Salvador Perez hits a walk-off single against the Oakland A's during the twelfth inning of the 2014 American League wild card game on September 30, 2016, at Kauffman Stadium. The Royals won 9-8 to earn their first postseason victory in twenty-nine years. (Courtesy *USA TODAY Sports/Peter G. Aiken*)

With Perez up, Colon dashed for second on a 1-2 count. The A's were ready and pitched out. But backup catcher Derek Norris dropped the ball, and Colon stood at second. It was the Royals' seventh steal of the game, which tied a postseason record. Two pitches later, Perez lunged and hit a slider past Donaldson for the winning run. The pitch to Perez was at least a foot out of the strike zone.

"Try two feet," Perez said with a laugh.

When Colon scored, the stadium shook for the second time of the night. The first was when James Shields took the mound for his warmup tosses before a crowd of 40,502. The Royals had gone 5-2 against the A's in the regular season, but both losses came after the A's acquired left-hander Jon Lester from Boston.

Lester had been a longtime nemesis of the Royals, throwing a no-hitter against them in 2008 with the Red Sox. Prior to the game, both managers figured it would be a low-scoring contest. Both managers were wrong.

Oakland's Brandon Moss hit a two-run home run off Shields in the first, and when Moss came to bat in the sixth with two on and nobody out, Royals manager Ned Yost wasn't about to let Shields face him again.

Yost inserted rookie right-hander Yordano Ventura, who had just started and thrown 73 pitches in the regular-season finale two days before. On the surface, the move was a curious one, as Ventura had only pitched out of the bullpen one other time all season, and that was the last game before the All-Star break. But Yost liked Ventura's power arm against Moss.

Ventura's first two fastballs were high so Perez came out to the mound. After their conversation, Moss whacked the next pitch—a 98 mph fastball—over the wall in center to give the A's a 5-3 lead. The home crowd was shocked, Yosted again by a manager who in their eyes seemed to bungle even the simplest of moves.

Shields gazed in disbelief from the dugout, and Ventura stayed in the game. He gave up another hit, threw a wild pitch, and got a fly-ball out before Yost had seen enough. As Yost walked to the mound, a chorus of boos followed his every step. Some fans couldn't wait for the game to be over, for in their minds it would be Yost's last as a Royal.

With Kelvin Herrera on the mound, the A's tacked on two more runs and led 7-3 at the end of six. Still down four in the eighth, things looked bleak for the Royals. But they still had hope.

"Everyone was saying something," Alex Gordon said. "The dugout was crazy. The energy in there, it felt like we were never down. We knew it was just one game, and when we got down, we just started fighting."

The Royals also had a secret weapon: Lester's left arm. Before the game, Royals first-base coach Rusty Kuntz, who is in charge of the team's running game, told the players a piece of well-kept information that is hard to fathom even to this day: Lester could not throw the ball to first base.

The last time Lester attempted to throw the ball to first before the wild-card game was April 30, 2013. Some Royals players didn't believe it. It just seemed too far-fetched to be true. The Royals actually wanted to test Lester in the first inning. After Hosmer walked, Butler singled to left to score Nori Aoki, and Hosmer took third. With Butler at first, the Royals called a double steal. With two strikes and Gordon at the plate, Butler drifted off first.

Lester saw Butler moving toward second but did not throw to first. He instead stepped off the mound. Hosmer was supposed to charge home but broke late, still not fully believing that Lester wouldn't throw the ball to first.

Lester threw awkwardly to shortstop Jed Lawrie near second, and with Butler caught in a slow rundown, Hosmer finally ran for home. A's catcher Geovany Soto tagged out Hosmer for the final out of the inning, but he hurt his thumb on the play—an injury that would loom large for the Royals in the hours to come.

With Soto out, the A's inserted Norris behind the plate. He was an All-Star that year, but for his bat and not his defense. So when opportunity to run arose in the eighth, Alcides Escobar swiped second easily and took third on a grounder.

Lorenzo Cain followed with a single to score Escobar. At first, Cain's lead grew bigger and bigger, but Lester still would not throw over. So on a 2-2 pitch to Hosmer, Cain sprinted for second and easily beat the tag. Hosmer walked, and A's manager Bob Melvin removed Lester with a 7-4 lead. As right-hander Luke Gregerson warmed up, the Royals coaching staff discussed whether they should hit the brakes with Lester out. They chose to floor it.

Facing Butler, Gregerson threw back-to-back sliders to open the at-bat. Butler punched the second one into right field, and Cain scored to make it 7-5. Butler was removed for Gore, perhaps the fastest man in baseball. Gore then stole second on the first pitch to Gordon. On Gregerson's next delivery, he bounced a breaking ball in the dirt. The ball rolled away past Norris, and Hosmer slid home to make it 7-6 heading to the ninth.

Closer Greg Holland worked out of a bases-loaded jam in the top half of the inning to give the Royals a chance against Oakland closer Sean Doolittle. Leading off the inning, Yost inserted veteran right-hander Josh Willingham to pinch-hit for Mike Moustakas. And when Willingham singled to right, the Royals had new life. They also had more speed.

Jarrod Dyson ran for Willingham and Escobar bunted him to second. With Aoki at the plate and a 2-1 count, Norris signaled for an inside pickoff move. Dyson saw it and didn't bite. It's rare that a pitcher will do back-to-back inside moves with a runner at second, and with that in mind, Dyson jetted for third on the next delivery.

Norris's throw was too late, and the Royals were a fly ball away from tying it. On the next pitch, Aoki flew out to right, and Dyson came home with the tying run, setting up the extra-inning dramatics. When Colon scored the game-winner in the twelfth, the noise was deafening.

"Obviously, I've been a part of some big ones in Tampa as well, but that game was one of the funnest I've ever been part of," Shields said.

While the team celebrated on the field, Archie Eversole's "We Ready," the song that became the team's anthem in the playoffs, blared as teammates swarmed Perez. Holland, meanwhile, ran around the diamond waving a giant Royals flag. The Royals had won a postseason game for the first time in twenty-nine years. The suffering was finally over, courtesy of one wild night.

"That's the most incredible game I've ever been a part of," Yost said after the game. "Our fans were unbelievable. Our guys never quit. When we fell behind there in the fifth, sixth inning, they kept battling back. They weren't going to be denied."

Blue October

10

Down Go the Halos

The Royals' dramatic wild-card win put them in the ALDS against the Angels, who had the best record in the AL at 98-64. The Angels also had Mike Trout, Albert Pujols, and 18-game-winner Jered Weaver. But the Royals had momentum and swept the series 3-0.

In Game One in Anaheim, the Royals won 3-2 in eleven innings on a home run by third baseman Mike Moustakas, a Los Angeles native and the team's No. 9 hitter. Moustakas's blast into the right-field seats was his first career postseason home run.

"As far as how big of a home run that is, that's probably the biggest one I've ever hit so far," Moustakas said after the game. "So it felt really amazing."

Danny Duffy got the win, pitching a scoreless inning in relief, and closer Greg Holland, who didn't get to the bullpen until the sixth inning after flying in from North Carolina for the birth of his son, Nash, pitched a 1-2-3 eleventh to earn his first career postseason save.

Kansas City Royals third baseman Mike Moustakas watches his home run during the eleventh inning against the Los Angeles Angels in Game One of the 2014 American League Divisional Series at Angel Stadium of Anaheim. (Courtesy *USA TODAY Sports/Robert Hanashiro*)

Holland's cross-country trip was anything but easy. First, he booked travel plans from the delivery room in Asheville, and his flight was delayed. Once he got to the ballpark on the West Coast, there were other issues.

"The guy that dropped me off did a great job getting me here," Holland said. "But he didn't really know where to go, and I didn't know where to go either. So I kind of made a few security guards nervous running up to them with a pack over my shoulder with my ID in my hand saying, 'I'm a player. I'm a player. Don't tackle me to the ground.'"

Security let Holland in, and he quickly got ready to pitch, finishing off the Royals' second postseason win in twenty-nine years. In 1985, Drew Saberhagen, Bret's son, was born during the World Series, and he and Holland grew up to be teammates at Western Carolina.

Holland, however, did not know that Drew had arrived as a postseason baby, just like his own son.

"[I've] never asked anyone how they entered the world," Holland quipped.

In Game Two, the Royals won 4-1 in eleven innings. This time Eric Hosmer was the hero. With one out, Lorenzo Cain legged out an infield hit, and Hosmer turned on the next pitch and deposited it into the seats in right field for a 3-1 lead.

Alex Gordon walked and stole second and advanced to third on a wild throw into center field. Gordon then scored on an infield hit by Salvador Perez for the final margin. Rookie Brandon Finnegan got the win, and Holland closed it out for the second night in a row.

Back in Kansas City for Game Three, there was no drama this time, as the Royals won 8-3 in nine innings. James Shields squared off against C.J. Wilson, and the Angels jumped out to a 1-0 lead in the first on a Trout home run. But the Royals answered with three runs in the bottom half of the inning off a bases-clearing double by Gordon that scored Nori Aoki, Cain, and Billy Butler.

Wilson didn't make it out of the first, and the Royals put the game out of reach early when Hosmer hit a two-run homer to center in the third and Moustakas capped it with a solo blast to right in the fourth. But the offensive highlight might have been when Butler stole second base in the third inning.

"I got the green light and made it happen," Butler said in another jubilant Royals clubhouse. "It was a great series, a great team effort out there. We won three in a row over those guys, and that's a great team, and it shows what type of team we have here."

Shields toughed out six innings, giving up two runs on six hits while striking out six. In the fifth, with two on and one out, Shields got a lift from Cain, who made back-to-back diving catches to end the inning.

Cain's sac fly in the fourth put the Royals up 7-2, and Aoki added an RBI single in the sixth. Kelvin Herrera pitched the seventh, Wade Davis the eighth, and Holland shut the door in the ninth, giving the hometown fans another October treat.

"To do it at home, and do this in front of our home crowd, it couldn't be any better," Hosmer said.

After the game, Hosmer tweeted out that he and several Royals were going to McFadden's—a popular bar in the Power and Light district in Kansas City—and he invited the fans to join them in the celebration. Hosmer and teammates bought fans drinks, splitting a $15,000 bar tab.

After the Royals won the division title in 1976, Royals legend George Brett recalled that like Hosmer, he bought some fans a drink. But there was one big difference.

"My bar bill was $25. It wasn't $20,000. I bought some fans a drink, but beer was a lot cheaper back then," Brett said with a laugh.

Raising Cain in the ALCS

Lorenzo Cain didn't play baseball until his sophomore season in high school. And he didn't crack the starting lineup until he was a senior. But during the 2014 ALCS against the Baltimore Orioles, Cain was the best player on the field.

Cain, the Royals center fielder, hit .533 (8-for-15) with five runs scored, two doubles, and an RBI and made several sparkling plays on defense and was named ALCS MVP after the Royals swept the Orioles in four games, the clincher a 2-1 win at Kauffman Stadium.

After an on-field celebration, the Royals took the party inside to the clubhouse. With plastic sheets covering their lockers, champagne and beer sprayed everywhere. A few minutes later, Cain walked in carrying his prize possession—the MVP award. But it wasn't in the open for long, as he pulled up the sheet that covered his locker and placed the trophy inside.

"It's too valuable!" Cain said just moments before teammate and close friend Salvador Perez poured champagne over his head.

The shower was fitting for both Cain and the Royals, who won their eighth straight game to start the postseason—an MLB record.

"To win eight straight and make history, and be a part of history is always a great feeling," Cain said.

A trip to the World Series and the MVP award capped a memorable week for Cain. In the span of just seven days, he became a father and joined Frank White (1980) and George Brett (1985) on the list of Royals to be named ALCS MVP.

The honor, however, wasn't the first MVP award of Cain's career. He was named MVP in the Arizona League his first year of pro ball in 2005 when he was in the Brewers organization. But he said that didn't compare.

"Coming into it, I definitely didn't think I would be MVP," Cain said. "I just do whatever it takes to put my teammates in position for us to score runs. I try to get on base as much as possible for guys to drive me in, and it's definitely worked out. But this is just a whole other level on a whole different stage than that was."

Kansas City Royals center fielder Lorenzo Cain hits a single against the Baltimore Orioles during the fourth inning in Game Three of the 2014 ALCS on October 14, 2014, in Kansas City, Missouri. Cain hit .533 and was named MVP. (Courtesy *USA TODAY Sports*/*John Rieger*)

The Brewers drafted Cain in the seventeenth round in 2004 after he played just one season at Tallahassee Community College in Florida. Cain then worked his way to the big leagues before being traded along with Alcides Escobar to the Royals for Zack Greinke.

"When it happened, it was definitely mixed emotions," Cain said. "But at the same time, it's a business. Trades happen, and being over here has been great. I'm definitely having a blast. As soon as I got here, I clicked with all the guys, and our chemistry is amazing. It's a fun group of guys and a talented group, as well."

Upon his arrival in Kansas City, the Royals gave the speedy outfielder Willie Wilson's famous No. 6.

"It's an honor to wear Willie's old number," Cain said. "Every time he sees me, he asks me to represent his number. I heard and saw that he was an amazing player when he played, so I'm just trying to be an all-around player, and that's exactly what he was."

Cain grew up in Madison, Florida. As a young boy, he had to help out around the house a lot because his mother, Patricia, was a single parent who worked two jobs—at Dillard's and a print shop—while raising Cain and his older brother after his father died when he was just four.

Cain's mother didn't have time to take her kids to practice, so Cain wasn't into baseball initially. His freshman year in high school he tried out for the basketball team and got cut. He made the baseball team the following year but didn't play much until his senior season.

In the minors, Cain played right field for a while before being shifted to center. There was a big learning curve, but he eventually learned things like reading the ball off the bat and how to properly turn his shoulder and close up when catching a fly ball.

Though sometimes Cain reminds fans of Wilson with his play, Cain patterns his game after Torii Hunter. In college, Cain studied the way Hunter swung the bat and played defense. On offense, Hunter would lean back when he swung, and Cain does that, as well.

"We call him the 'Lean Back Kid,'" said speedster Jarrod Dyson. "On every swing he leans back. He doesn't try to pimp nothing, that's just his normal swing. And we kind of love it when he leans back."

Cain and Perez, meanwhile, have a unique relationship. For years, Perez has made a habit of posting photos and videos of himself and Cain interacting on social media, and Perez isn't planning on stopping anytime soon.

"That's my boy," Perez said of Cain. "That's my younger brother. Everything I do with him is something fun. He's always laughing. He's a guy that likes to smile on camera, that's why I pick him."

At 6-foot-2, 205 pounds, Cain is a pretty big guy himself. And with Perez at 6-4 and 240 pounds, the Royals seemed big enough to hold their own in any fight. And the sweep of the O's put the Royals in the World Series for the first time since 1985. But a Giant test would await.

Ninety Feet Short

All that separated the Royals from the 2014 World Series title was 90 feet. With two out in the bottom of the ninth of Game Seven at Kauffman Stadium, Alex Gordon stood at the plate facing Giants ace Madison Bumgarner representing the tying run.

Just three days earlier, the big left-hander devoured the Royals for the second time in the Series with a four-hit shutout in Game Five. This time, however,

Bumgarner was trying to finish off a five-inning save when Gordon stepped into the batter's box. On Bumgarner's second pitch, Gordon hit an 87 mph slider to the gap in left-center field.

The hopes of a generation that had known nothing but losing were lifted. When Giants center fielder Gregor Blanco misplayed the ball and it rolled all the way to the wall, and when left fielder Juan Perez couldn't field it cleanly, Gordon advanced to third, sending the crowd into a frenzy as their championship dreams were one base from reality.

Surely, with Salvador Perez—the hero of the wild-card game—coming up, he would get a hit and Gordon would score the tying run, and the Royals would somehow win and twenty-nine years of pain and despair would somehow be wiped away with a World Series title. But as rewarding as October can be, it can be equally cruel. Gordon never advanced another foot, as Perez fouled out to third baseman Pablo Sandoval near the Giants dugout for the final out, and the Royals lost 3-2, ending a magical run a short distance from the throne.

"Losing the ballgame by 90 feet is tough," Royals manager Ned Yost said after the game. "But the hard part about this is that you work all year to climb to the top of the mountain, and then boom, you fall back, and you've got to start right back at the bottom again next year.

"But we've gained a ton of experience. I don't think I've ever been as proud of anything in my life as I have been of this team, and the way they performed this postseason. It was just fantastic."

Many Royals fans believe third-base coach Mike Jirschele should have sent Gordon home. But replays show that barring an errant throw from shortstop Brandon Crawford, Gordon would have been out by a good 30 feet.

"I'm not that fast, and I kind of stumbled around second a little bit," Gordon said after the loss. "I was trying to score as hard as I could, and he made a good stop stopping me at third."

Technically, the game-winning run came in the fourth when Michael Morse's single off Kelvin Herrera scored Sandoval to break a 2-2 tie, but the outcome was pretty much decided the second Bumgarner walked out of the bullpen gate.

Bumgarner, the winning pitcher in Game One and Game Five, gave up two hits, struck out four, and walked none in Game Seven and was named MVP after posting a 0.43 ERA in 21 innings. The Giants scored two runs off starter Jeremy Guthrie in the second, but the Royals answered in the bottom half of the inning against Giants starter Tim Hudson when Billy Butler hit a leadoff single and Gordon doubled him home from first. Perez was then hit by a pitch, and after Mike

San Francisco Giants players celebrate on the field after defeating the Kansas City Royals 3-2 in Game Seven of the World Series on October 29, 2014, at Kauffman Stadium. That's Royals third-base coach Mike Jirschele trotting off the field. (Courtesy *USA TODAY Sports/Peter G. Aiken*)

Moustakas advanced Gordon to third, Omar Infante's sac fly tied it. But that was all the offense the Royals would get.

Jeremy Affeldt, the former Royal who was part of a lot of losing in Kansas City, got the win in relief. Guthrie took the loss, giving up three runs in 3 ⅓ innings a night after Royals rookie Yordano Ventura threw seven shutouts innings to force Game Seven.

Though the Royals' ride did not culminate with a championship like the 1985 team, they accomplished something equally important. They brought hope and playoff baseball back to a fan base that had suffered so much.

"I couldn't be more proud to be associated with this group of men," Butler said. "It's unfortunate that we fell a bit short, but we have nothing to be ashamed of. We left it all out there."

As the Giants celebrated near the mound, Gordon walked back to the dugout with his hands on his helmet. With each difficult step, he could hear the cheers from the Giants' dogpile.

But then Gordon heard something else. An old familiar chant broke out from the stands.

"Let's go, Royals!"

Quiet at first, the chant—a heartfelt thank-you from the fans—quickly echoed throughout the stadium.

Winter had finally arrived, but baseball was back in Kansas City.

11

Unfinished Business

Yost in a Class by Himself

Ned Yost used to go to coffee shops in Kansas City, and the name "Frank" would be called out when a particular order was ready. Yost would then go to the counter and pick up his order. No, Edgar Frederick "Ned" Yost didn't change his name. He just used Frank as an alias in public back when his team was one of the worst in baseball.

Yost doesn't have to take such drastic measures anymore to conceal his identity, as he is now the Royals' all-time winningest manager with 549 wins entering the 2017 season.

"It's nice, but I don't really look at it as an individual achievement," Yost said. "First of all, I don't feel like I'm in the same class as Whitey Herzog and Dick Howser. And two, it's an organizational achievement. It starts with our scouts that work their tails off trying to find these kids and sign them, and then to our player development people and major league coaches that mentor them through all the ups and downs to get them to a point where they can be a championship team."

Ned Yost became manager of the Kansas City Royals in 2010 and is now the team's all-time winningest manager. Since his arrival, Yost has brought energy and a steady hand to the team from the dugout. (Courtesy *Jeff Deters*)

When Yost, who passed Howser (404) and Herzog (410) for wins in the summer of 2015, was hired to replace Trey Hillman as manager on May 13, 2010, the thought that the Royals could win a championship again was somewhere between never and keep dreaming. The Royals were still a laughingstock, and the hiring itself had mixed reviews.

In 2008, Yost guided the Brewers to an 83-67 record but was fired with twelve games to go, as his team was on a downhill spiral in late September and was in danger of missing the playoffs. The Brewers ultimately made the postseason, but Yost had to watch from afar. He then returned home to his farm outside Atlanta and was out of baseball in 2009.

Royals general manager Dayton Moore, who worked with Yost when they were with the Braves, then called and offered him a job as an adviser in the front office in January 2010. In spring training, Yost got to see the likes of Mike Moustakas, Eric Hosmer, and Salvador Perez up close. Yost had already seen Lorenzo Cain and Alcides Escobar when he was manager of the Brewers, so he knew the Royals were going to be stocked with talent in the near future.

Upon his arrival, Yost immediately brought a new energy to the franchise that is still felt today.

"Ned's a tremendous leader, a tremendous competitor, he works extremely well with our entire front office, and it's an honor for us that he's the all-time winningest manager in Royals history," Moore said.

One of Yost's greatest strengths is delivering his message through positive reinforcement even when players are struggling. Escobar knows this firsthand.

"He's always positive," Escobar said. "This team has a lot of energy, and he's always right there. He keeps us playing hard and tells us to enjoy the game."

The Royals certainly do that, and Perez, who probably has the most fun of anybody on the field, credits Yost for a lot of the good times.

"He is great to play for," Perez said. "I'm so happy he's my manager. We want to win for him and the fans. He makes us play hard and encourages us and lets us have fun."

Yost's tenure as manager has been an evolution of change. In August 2014, while the Royals were still fighting for a playoff spot, Yost upset many fans by commenting on how there were a few too many empty seats following a walk-off home win against Minnesota. This only gave fans even more ammo, since he was already in their crosshairs for his surprising lineup cards and questionable in-game decisions. During the 2014 playoffs, the *Wall Street Journal* even called him a dunce.

Yost ultimately got the last laugh, and the respect of the national media, but it wasn't easy. Even when dealing with the local media in those days, Yost would sometimes get defensive if a question wasn't to his liking. But since the 2014 playoffs, Yost seemingly has turned over a new leaf.

Yost initially was a stickler to his old-school ways, having learned the trade from spending twelve seasons as an assistant in Atlanta with Bobby Cox. But over the years, Yost has adapted to the new culture of today's game. He had to. His survival in many ways depended on it.

Yost is a big NASCAR fan. He wears No. 3 in honor of his late friend Dale Earnhardt. He's friends with comedian Jeff Foxworthy, who also owns land near

Yost's farm in Georgia. Together, they helped form a hunting group called the "Thump Monkeys."

"He's kind of laid back," Jarrod Dyson once said. "But he's real serious about the game of baseball."

Yost also is a big fan of country music, but initially he would not allow music to be played in the clubhouse. Cox wouldn't allow it, so neither would Yost. But eventually, Yost let his team play music, including Latin, partly because the team has several players from Latin America, but more so because the game has changed, and Yost has, too.

"I think it finally got to a point in these kids' second year where I realized these guys are different, they're from a different generation than I grew up," Yost said. "It doesn't mean that it's right or it's wrong, but it's who they are. And I think in order to have success you have to allow them to be who they are."

Yost also started letting the team have celebrations in the clubhouse when appropriate, and he made the decision to let the players police the locker room themselves instead of doing it himself.

Also, instead of tightening his grip, Yost loosened the reigns with his coaching staff and began to trust and value their opinions more. Yost's rise to the top of the team's win list mirrors that of the organization in recent years. Yost's 2010 team went 67-95 and finished last in the division. They haven't finished last since.

The job Yost has done from the Royals dugout has truly been remarkable, especially when you consider that when Herzog and Howser took over, those Royals teams were already built to win and Yost was tasked with bringing a franchise back to life that in many ways was on life support.

When Yost's career is over, he will someday be in the Royals Hall of Fame, and his number very well could be retired. But that's not important right now to Yost, who is still enjoying the ride.

"This team is wonderful to be around," Yost said. "It's a joy to be their manager, it really is."

The Magnificent Seven

In 2014, the Royals became America's Team with their run to the World Series. In 2015, their popularity was just as strong, as seven Royals were selected to the All-Star Game on July 14 in Cincinnati.

Alcides Escobar, Lorenzo Cain, Salvador Perez, and Alex Gordon were voted in by the fans as starters, while relievers Kelvin Herrera and Wade Davis were selected as reserves by manager Ned Yost. Third baseman Mike Moustakas was the final

AL Fan Vote winner with 19.3 million votes. Escobar, Cain, Herrera, Davis, and Moustakas all were first-time selections.

"These people are such loyal fans and such great fans," Moustakas said after his selection. "It's just overwhelming to see 19.3 million votes. Every one of those guys I was up against deserves to be there, too. They're great ballplayers and had great seasons. And I just want to say thank you to all the fans in Kansas City that made this happen for me. It's really special."

Moustakas, after struggling as a young player, put together a solid first half. He hit .297 with seven home runs and 31 RBIs while batting second. Moustakas thanked Yost and general manager Dayton Moore for never giving up on him despite a demotion to the minors in 2014.

"Even when I was doubting myself, Ned wasn't," Moustakas said. "And Dayton wasn't either, and they continued to stick with me and it helped me a lot."

Escobar, after struggling at the plate early in his career, hit .290 in the leadoff spot, while Cain hit .316 with eight home runs and 42 RBIs. Perez hit .262 with 15 homers and 38 RBIs, while Herrera had a 1.95 ERA as a seventh-inning reliever and Davis had a minuscule 0.46 ERA and nine saves in 39 innings.

Though the seven selections were a franchise record, Gordon didn't make the trip. He hit .279 with 11 homers and 38 RBIs and had a .394 OBP in the first half but suffered a severe groin strain a few days earlier and had to sit out for the second year in a row with an injury.

Another Royal was a victim of somewhat bad timing despite being quite popular in the polls. Omar Infante, the team's starting second baseman, was struggling to keep his batting average above the .200 mark the whole first half, but for a while the #VoteOmar movement worked on social media, and he was the leading vote-getter at second base until Houston's Jose Altuve *somehow* passed him late in the process.

For Yost, it was his sixth All-Star Game as a coach and first as a manager. The AL All-Stars won 6-3, giving the AL home-field advantage throughout the playoffs. Cain had two hits and an RBI, while Escobar had a hit in two at-bats. Davis pitched a scoreless eighth inning and struck out two.

Here's Johnny!

The Royals had the best record in the AL, and a division title was likely going to be theirs even if they had simply held their cards at the trade deadline.

Still, scouts were dispatched all across the country as general manager Dayton Moore knew winning a World Series would take more than what the Royals had on their roster. The starting rotation was leaking oil, and the Alex Gordon injury left the team thin on the bench.

The Royals focused in on two players to fill those holes: Cincinnati Reds pitcher Johnny Cueto and Oakland's Ben Zobrist. Cueto was the biggest soon-to-be free agent on the trading block. The Royals had some interest in Detroit ace left-hander David Price, but the Tigers were still hoping for a wild card, and Price wasn't available at the time.

The Royals had their eye on Cueto since the previous winter, when they identified him as a potential trade candidate. With that in mind, the Royals sent scouts to each of Cueto's starts for at least two months before they acquired him in late July in what was the biggest trade in Royals history. To get him, the Royals traded Brandon Finnegan, John Lamb, and Cody Reed, three young left-handed pitchers. But with the acquisition of Cueto, the Royals now had a legitimate ace with whom they could match up in the postseason.

"He was a top priority for us," Moore said after the deal was announced. "We felt he fit us and that he was a pitcher that matched up very well with anybody."

At the time of the deal, Cueto was 7-6 with a 2.62 ERA in 19 starts for a struggling Reds team that was on its way to a last-place finish. Cueto was an All-Star in 2014, when he won 20 games, and he was a 19-game winner in 2012.

Also at the time of the trade, Yordano Ventura was struggling, left-hander Jason Vargas was lost for the season with Tommy John surgery, and Chris Young was dealing with a bad back. So Moore had little choice but to make the move for Cueto.

The Cueto trade gave Moore the pitcher the Royals needed to win the pennant and World Series, but it also showed how far the Royals had come as a franchise. The Royals, who were a laughingstock for years and once the biggest seller at the trade deadline, were now pulling off a trade that could help them win their first title in thirty years.

Moore, however, wasn't done dealing. He needed more depth and versatility offensively. And a couple days after acquiring Cueto, Moore traded for Zobrist, one of the game's most versatile players and another soon-to-be free agent.

Zobrist began his tenure as a Royal filling in for Gordon in left field. But Omar Infante continued to struggle at second base and at the plate and later suffered a season-ending quad injury. So Zobrist took over at second base and also became a force in the two-hole. But while Zobrist was an instant hit, things wouldn't come as easily for Cueto.

12

Reclaiming the Crown

Central Standard Time

The Royals accomplished the first order of business for the 2015 season, winning the AL Central for the first time in team history with a 10-4 win over Seattle on September 24 at Kauffman Stadium.

"It's very special," Royals manager Ned Yost said on the field just moments after the final out. "There's like 25 guys on this team that weren't even born the last time the Royals won a championship. And to be able to do it in front of our fans, you guys have been fantastic all year long. You're right there with us every pitch, we can't do it without you. Thank you so much!"

It was the Royals' seventh division title in team history and first since 1985, when they won the AL West.

Johnny Cueto got the win, pitching seven innings of three-run ball. In typical Royals fashion, they had to rally to win it. The Royals trailed 3-2 when they came to bat in the fifth but tied it on a homer by Eric Hosmer. The Royals then took the

Kansas City Royals players celebrate after defeating the Seattle Mariners 10-4 to win the American League Central for the first time in team history on September 24, 2015, at Kauffman Stadium. (Courtesy *USA TODAY Sports/John Rieger*)

lead for good in the sixth when Lorenzo Cain's two-out single scored Alex Gordon and Ben Zobrist.

"It's a great feeling," Hosmer said of winning the division title. "Leaving spring training, this is the goal, to win the division and get back to the postseason. We got a lot of work left. This is step one, but we're going to enjoy this one."

Mike Moustakas went 3-for-3 with a home run, three RBIs, and three runs scored.

"We never gave up, we never stopped, kept playing hard," Moustakas said. "You can't say enough about every guy on this team. They came out every single day ready to play."

The victory also ensured that veteran outfielder Alex Rios would finally get to play in the postseason for the first time.

"This is something that I've been looking to do my whole career, and I finally got to do it with this team and that's awesome," Rios said. "It was something that I thought about when I went through in free agency and it was a good choice."

The win also put twenty-nine-year-old rookie outfielder Paulo Orlando in the postseason for the first time.

"I'm pretty excited for the playoffs," said Orlando, who spent ten years in the minors. "We were very fortunate to do a good job this year, like they did last year. We started pretty good this season and just never stopped playing hard. We just tried to give 100 percent, and that's what we'll do in the playoffs, and that's going to be neat to see."

In the celebration in the clubhouse, Royals left-hander Danny Duffy stood next to FSKC host Joel Goldberg, who was wearing a 2015 KC Postseason hat. Duffy, however, was wearing something a little more extravagant.

"What are you wearing?" Goldberg asked.

"I'm wearing a bear suit, Joel," Duffy said with a smile.

The Royals went on to finish the regular season with a 95-67 record, capturing home-field advantage throughout the playoffs when they beat the Twins 6-1 on the last day of the regular season, coupled with a Toronto loss.

Houston, We Don't Have a Problem

Many in the Royals organization wanted to play the Yankees in the ALDS. They wanted this not so much because they believed the Royals matched up better against the Bronx Bombers than they did against the Houston Astros, but because it had more to do with the fact that they wanted payback for the 1976 through 1978 losses in the ALCS.

But the Royals never got that chance because the Astros beat the Yankees in the wild-card game at Yankee Stadium. The Astros were trying to duplicate what the Royals had done a year earlier by riding the momentum of the win in the wild card all the way to the World Series. And if it weren't for another historic Royal rally, and the pitching of Johnny Cueto, they might have done it.

Trailing 2-1 in the best-of-five series and on the brink of elimination, the Royals trailed 6-2 in the top of the eighth in Game Four at Houston. But the Royals rallied for five runs in the eighth en route to a 9-6 win before Cueto fired them to a 7-2 victory in Game Five at Kauffman Stadium.

In Game Four, the Royals trailed 3-2 in the seventh, but the Astros scored three times off reliever Ryan Madson to take the 6-2 lead. Inside Minute Maid Park, the noise was deafening.

The plans for the celebration in the Astros locker room also were being made, and the Twitter account for Texas Governor Greg Abbott offered congratulations to the Astros for "advancing to the ALCS!"

When the Royals returned to the dugout with their season down to six outs, Mike Moustakas made a bold prediction.

"We're not losing this game!" he shouted.

Moustakas has always been a fiery player, and when he speaks, people listen. Fueled by his Moose call, the Royals, who had just two hits the first seven innings, strung together five straight singles—four against Houston reliever Will Harris—to give the Royals hope. Alex Rios started it with a base hit to left, and Alcides Escobar and Ben Zobrist followed with hits to center. With the bases loaded, Lorenzo Cain singled to left field, scoring Rios.

Astros manager A.J. Hinch summoned left-hander Tony Sipp from the bullpen to face Eric Hosmer, and Hosmer hit a line drive to right to score Escobar, cutting the deficit to 6-4. Two pitches later, switch-hitting Kendrys Morales hit a ball that bounced off the mound, and rookie shortstop Carlos Correa came in to field the double-play ball.

Correa had swatted two home runs already in the game, and a simple catch and throw to second base could have turned things around quickly for the Astros and dashed any hopes the Royals had. But the ball glanced off his glove and rolled into center field. From hero to goat the youngster became in an instant, while Zobrist and Cain scored to tie it a 6-6. With one out, Drew Butera came up to bat. Butera entered in the bottom of the seventh after Salvador Perez reached in the top of the frame and was replaced by pinch-runner Terrance Gore.

Hinch inserted closer Luke Gregerson—the same Luke Gregerson who faced the Royals in the wild-card game a year earlier—to face Butera. In Butera's first postseason at-bat, the backup catcher won the ten-pitch battle, reaching on a walk to bring up Alex Gordon.

Gordon then hit a grounder to second that scored Hosmer for the go-ahead run.

Ball game.

"That was an unbelievable inning," Royals manager Ned Yost said after the game.

"I can't explain it," Gordon said.

Kansas City Royals pitcher Johnny Cueto celebrates after retiring the Houston Astros in the eighth inning in Game Five of the ALDS on October 14, 2015, at Kauffman Stadium. Cueto pitched eight strong innings and retired the last nineteen batters he faced. (Courtesy *USA TODAY Sports/Denny Medley*)

Hosmer added a two-run blast in the ninth for the final margin, and Cueto two nights later put the Royals in the ALCS for the second year in a row. The right-hander, who was disappointing at times during the regular season, dazzled, showing why the July trade was worth the price. Cueto struck out eight in eight innings.

"I woke up today on the right foot," Cueto said through an interpreter after the game. "As soon as I woke up, I felt something magical that this was Game Five and I had to show up for everybody, for my team and the fans."

Behind an electric crowd of 40,566, Cueto silenced the Houston bats, except for a two-run home run in the second inning. But he was untouchable after that and retired his last nineteen batters.

Houston's baggage from Game Four finally made it to Kansas City in the fifth inning, when the Royals scored three runs. Down 2-1 to start the fifth, Rios hit a two-run double to score Salvador Perez and Gordon, giving the Royals the lead for good. And Morales capped the night with a three-run homer in the eighth off Dallas Keuchel, the Houston ace and AL Cy Young winner who dominated Game Three and put the Astros one win away from the ALCS only to be denied by the Royals thanks to another rally for the ages, and Cueto.

"There's no doubt that Game Four was an inspiration to me," Cueto said. "To see Moose screaming at everybody in the dugout like we're not done yet, all I kept thinking about was if we came back to win this game, I'll take care of business in Game Five."

He certainly did.

The Great Escape

The clouds moved closer and closer to Kauffman Stadium. The rain was coming. Royals manager Ned Yost was hoping to get through the eighth inning of Game Six of the ALCS against Toronto without having to use closer Wade Davis.

Davis had been spectacular in the role since he replaced Greg Holland, who was lost for the season with Tommy John surgery late in the year. The situation Yost was faced with was exactly what he was hoping to avoid, but Davis and the Royals prevailed 4-3 to advance to their second straight World Series.

The Royals were up 3-1 when the eighth inning started, and Yost sent setup man Ryan Madson to the mound. Yost was hoping for a quick inning, as he knew the rain would be falling in just a few minutes and the game would surely be delayed thirty minutes or so.

Davis was on call for the eighth, so he knew he might have to come in and get out of a jam, if needed, as Madson was set to face the top of the Toronto order. Yost, meanwhile, knew if he used Davis in the eighth, he might not be available for the ninth because of the pending rain delay.

From the dugout, Yost watched as Madson gave up a leadoff single to Ben Revere before striking out Josh Donaldson. But two pitches later, Toronto slugger Jose Bautista turned on a fastball that landed in the seats in left field, tying it at 3-3. After Madson walked Edwin Encarnacion, Yost handed the ball to Davis. He had no choice.

Kansas City's Wade Davis celebrates with catcher Salvador Perez after the Royals defeated the Toronto Blue Jays in Game Six of the ALCS on October 23, 2015, at Kauffman Stadium. After coming on in the eighth inning and sitting through a forty-five minute rain delay, Davis stayed on for the ninth and got out of a jam to send the Royals to their second straight World Series. (Courtesy *USA TODAY Sports/Denny Medley*)

"I got to bring Wade in the ballgame right there just to hold it," Yost said after the game.

Davis escaped without further damage. But then a forty-five minute rain delay halted play in the middle of the eighth. In the bowels of the stadium, Davis rode an exercise bike to keep his legs warm. He played catch with Drew Butera in the tunnel to stay loose.

As the delay wore on, his teammates wondered if he could pitch the ninth. Even Davis himself wondered if he could do it.

"I wasn't sure," Davis said.

Dayton Moore made his way downstairs. Yost and the coaching staff discussed the possibility of using Davis in the ninth, and Moore knew what the answer would be. When Yost sent Davis back out for the ninth, there was still some concern in his own mind until Holland put Yost's mind at ease.

"Don't worry about nothing," Holland told Yost. "Wade wants to go to the World Series."

In the ninth, Davis was pitching with a one-run lead after the Royals scored in the bottom of the eighth. But had the delay lasted even just a few minutes longer, Davis might not have been able to pitch.

"If it would have went a little bit long, maybe," Davis said.

After the rain passed and the infield was deemed playable, the Royals went to work. Cain drew a leadoff walk and scored from first on Eric Hosmer's single down the right-field line. Bautista fielded the ball a few feet in front of the foul line, and Royals third-base coach Mike Jirschele watched to see if he would make the same mistake again. He did.

Earlier in the series with a runner at first on a similar play, Jirschele noticed Bautista threw to second base. That time, Kendrys Morales was on first. This time it was Cain. So when Bautista fielded the ball and spun toward second, the door opened for Cain to try to score.

"I just kept going," Cain said. "I gave it all I had. I didn't think he was going to send me, but I turned it on."

Cain, who was not running on the pitch, raced around third and slid home, giving the Royals a 4-3 lead.

In Game Seven of the 2014 World Series, Jirschele made the decision to hold Alex Gordon at third base. He has been criticized many times since, but it was the right call then, and sending Cain proved to be the right call, as well.

So with a one-run lead, how did Davis feel when he took the mound for the ninth when he had last pitched an hour earlier?

"I felt fine," Davis said.

But Davis initially wasn't fine. He gave up a hit to catcher Russell Martin on his first pitch, and Blue Jays manager John Gibbons inserted pinch-runner Dalton Pompey, who stole second and third. Kevin Pillar walked and later stole second on a strikeout. But Davis struck out Revere and got Donaldson to ground out to third to end it, giving the Royals the AL pennant once again.

Davis, who rarely shows emotion on the mound, screamed after the final out, threw his glove into the air, and jumped into the arms of Salvador Perez as the team celebrated on the mound.

"What he did was legendary tonight," Royals pitcher Danny Duffy said. "That's the best word I can give for you to describe it. That's going to go down as one of the most impressive performances I've ever seen."

The last time Davis had pitched after a rain delay was when he was a starting pitcher with Tampa Bay. When he came on for the ninth, while he felt fine, he could tell something was missing. Davis, though, soon found it.

"I picked up some more adrenaline," Davis said. "With the delay, I think I lost some, but I felt pretty strong after that."

For the second time in the series, the Royals had bested David Price, the rent-a-player the Blue Jays acquired before the trade deadline to bolster their rotation for the stretch run. After winning 5-0 in Game One, the Royals trailed 3-0 in the bottom of the seventh in Game Two against Price. Price gave up a leadoff hit to Alcides Escobar on his first pitch of the game, then retired the next eighteen batters. But the Royals rallied for five runs off Price in the seventh inning as Hosmer, Morales, Mike Moustakas, Gordon, and Alex Rios all had RBIs in the 6-3 win.

The rally began when Ben Zobrist started the inning with a popper that landed between Bautista and second baseman Ryan Goins. Goins called Bautista off with his hand but then stopped. Bautista, meanwhile, had already stopped seconds before, and the ball hit the ground, giving the Royals the crease they needed.

In Game Three in Toronto, Johnny Cueto was rocked for eight runs in two innings, and the Royals lost 11-8. In Game Four, the Royals rolled to a 14-2 win in which Escobar had two hits and four RBIs. The Blue Jays sent the series back to Kansas City with a 7-1 win in Game Five before Davis finished it in Game Six.

"He's the best," said Escobar, who was named ALCS MVP after hitting .478 in the series. "He's the best."

Let It Reign

Only the Royals can turn the impossible into the probable and do it with such grace. Night after night, game after game, the Royals trailed in the late innings, so when they were down two runs to the New York Mets in the ninth inning in Game Five of the World Series on November 1, 2015, at Citi Field in New York, it was really no surprise. Nor was the finish—a 7-2 victory in 12 innings that gave the Royals their first World Series championship since 1985.

In the thick of it was Eric Hosmer and Christian Colon, the last man on the roster. Hosmer scored the tying run in the ninth, and Colon, in his first at-bat of the postseason, singled in the go-ahead run in a five-run twelfth.

Finished business.

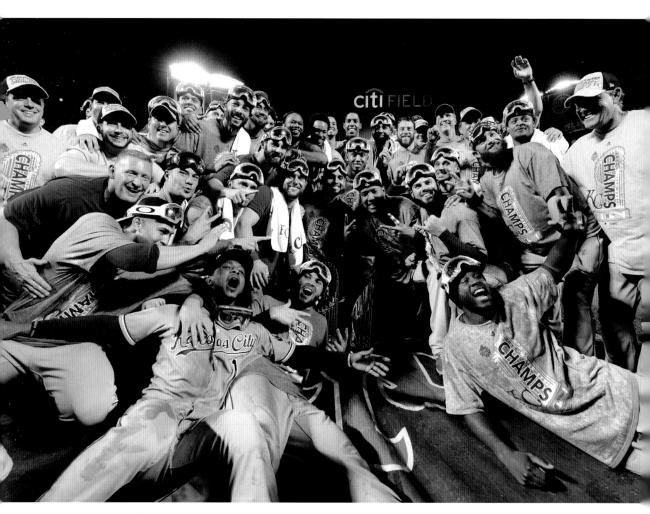

The Kansas City Royals celebrate on the mound after defeating the New York Mets 7-2 in twelve innings in Game Five of the World Series on November 1, 2015, at Citi Field in New York. The victory gave the Royals their first title in thirty years. (Courtesy *USA TODAY Sports/Jeff Curry*)

"From Day One there was no doubt in my mind that they wouldn't accomplish it," Royals manager Ned Yost said after the game. "There was no doubt in their mind that they wouldn't accomplish it."

A year after Alex Gordon was left stranded at third base on the final out in Game Seven of the World Series, Hosmer couldn't wait any longer. He had to go home—from third on a ground ball that was just a few feet in front of him.

Hosmer had just doubled in Lorenzo Cain off Mets starter Matt Harvey to cut the deficit to 2-1 in the ninth. Mets manager Terry Collins went to closer Jeurys Familia, who had blown two saves already in the series. A similar horror script soon followed for the Mets.

After a groundout, Hosmer took third. And with Salvador Perez at the plate, Hosmer took his lead on a 1-0 delivery from Familia. Perez hit a grounder to the hole between shortstop and third. Mets third baseman David Wright took a few steps to his left, cutting the ball off from Wilmer Flores.

Hosmer froze on contact, but while his feet were motionless, his mind raced back to a conversation he had with Rusty Kuntz. Before Game One, the Royals advanced scouts informed the coaches that Wright had changed his throwing motion from over the top to sidearm because of a bad back. They also told them that Mets first baseman Lucas Duda had trouble throwing the ball anywhere on the diamond.

As soon as the ball left Wright's fingertips, Hosmer charged home. A good throw from first probably would have gotten him at the plate. But Duda's throw sailed past catcher Travis d'Arnaud and hit the backstop, and Hosmer slid home safely with the tying run.

"Whoo!" Hosmer yelled as he jumped back up.

"There's a bunch of base-running plays that go on throughout the year that people don't really see. Of course, they'll remember that one," Mike Moustakas said. "But he can go first to third, tagging up on a ball in center field, things like that. I think he's becoming an all-around great player, and it's awesome to watch. He's someone that you come to the field to watch play the game, and he plays it right."

In the twelfth with the score still tied 2-2, Colon stepped in to pinch-hit for Luke Hochevar. Perez started the inning with a single, and Jarrod Dyson came on as a pinch-runner. Second base would soon be Dyson's on a steal, and he took third on a groundout.

Colon then singled to left off Mets reliever Addison Reed and Dyson scored, giving the Royals the lead for good. A year earlier in the wild-card game against Oakland, Colon had the game-tying hit and scored the game-winning run.

"Sometimes I find myself trying to remember how exactly it all went down because it all happened so fast, kind of like the wild-card game," Colon said of his World Series at-bat. "I just remember skip coming up to me and saying I was hitting third.

"I got super pumped up. I went and grabbed my bat and I was ready to hit. And I step out there, and I was like, 'Whoa!' It's packed, we're in New York, we're not at Kauffman. It was a cool experience, and I had to treat it like a normal game and a normal at-bat."

Kansas City first baseman Eric Hosmer slides home with the tying run past New York Mets catcher Travis d'Arnaud in the ninth inning in Game Five of the World Series at Citi Field. Hosmer's mad dash from third came on a fielder's choice just a few feet in front of him at third base. Mets first baseman Lucas Duda threw wildly to home plate, and had he made an accurate throw, Hosmer likely would have been out. Instead, the Royals rallied and became World Series champs. (Courtesy *USA TODAY Sports/Jeff Curry*)

The first two at-bats of Colon's postseason career, however, were anything but normal. They were two of the biggest hits in Royals history, and he went 2-for-2 with two RBIs.

"He's a winner," Yost said. "And you put him in a situation, and he's going to give you everything that he's got."

Colon made the 2015 Opening Day roster and got his first chance to be a starter when shortstop Alcides Escobar went on the disabled list with a concussion in April. Colon later played third when Moustakas went on leave to be with his dying mother. Somewhat caught in a numbers game, Colon was later optioned to Triple-A before returning in September so he could be on the playoff roster.

"I've had a chance to go back and really think about what we accomplished as a team," Colon said. "And Game Five, I've seen the highlights. And every single time I look at them I can't help but to think about how we came together to come back in that game.

"This team is just built to come back, and the relentlessness that we have is unreal, and I'm very proud to be associated with this team."

In Game Five, Colon later scored on a double by Escobar, and Cain cleared the bases with another double to put it out of reach. And when Wade Davis struck out Flores looking, the Royals were crowned once again.

They certainly wouldn't have reached that pinnacle without Edinson Volquez. The right-hander was the team's most consistent starter during the season, and he had just returned from his father's funeral to start Game Five.

Kansas City's Christian Colon celebrates after hitting an RBI single against the New York Mets in the twelfth inning in Game Five of the World Series at Citi Field. A year after getting the game-tying hit and scoring the winning run in the wild-card game against Oakland, Colon's single against the Mets broke a 2-2 tie, and the Royals went on to win the game 7-2 to earn their first World Series title in thirty years. (Courtesy *USA TODAY Sports/Brad Penner*)

Volquez started Game One against Harvey, and just minutes before the first pitch, news leaked out that his father had died in the Dominican Republic at age sixty-three because of complications of a heart condition.

Volquez's wife called Dayton Moore with the bad news, and she asked that the club not tell Volquez until after his start. The Royals complied, and Volquez threw six quality innings. The death of Volquez's father was the third death of a family member on the Royals team, following the passing of Moustakas's mother and Chris Young's father.

In this age of social media, Yost thought there was a chance Volquez could somehow find out about his father's death while Game One was going on. So he had a contingency plan in place, and that plan was to hand the ball to Young.

Young pitched the final three innings and got the win as the Royals won 5-4 in fourteen innings in a game that was the longest in World Series history, taking 5 hours, 9 minutes to complete.

The Royals scored the game-winner when Hosmer's sac fly scored Escobar, who led off the game with an inside-the-park-home run on Harvey's first pitch.

Kansas City Royals catcher Salvador Perez (right) and owner David Glass celebrate with the Commissioners Trophy after the Royals defeated the New York Mets in Game Five of the World Series at Citi Field. Perez hit .364 and was named MVP. (Courtesy *USA TODAY Sports/Al Bello/Pool Photo*)

The Royals trailed 4-3 in the ninth when Familia took the mound, but the series changed when Gordon's dramatic game-tying homer to center field gave the Royals new life. After the game, Volquez was already bound for the Dominican before the clubhouse opened to the media.

In Game Two, the Royals rolled to a 7-1 win, as Johnny Cueto threw a complete game and walked off the field to chants of "Johnny! Johnny!" from the hometown crowd, making the final memory of baseball at Kauffman Stadium that season a great one.

The Royals lost 9-3 in Game Three. Prior to the first pitch, Mets starter Noah Syndergaard said he had "a few tricks" up his sleeve for the Royals. On his first pitch, Syndergaard threw a 98 mph fastball at Escobar's head.

The pitch immediately infuriated the Royals. From the dugout, Moustakas barked at Syndergaard, and in the clubhouse following the loss, the team continued to voice displeasure.

"That's not good," Escobar said.

"It was weak," Alex Rios said.

"I think the whole team is pretty upset," Moustakas said. "The first pitch of the game goes whizzing by our leadoff hitter's head. All twenty-five guys in that dugout are pretty fired up."

The Royals won 5-3 in Game Four, as Daniel Murphy's flaw and a three-run eighth put the team one win away from the title. The Royals' comeback began with consecutive one-out walks, forcing Collins to insert Familia for a five-out save. Hosmer promptly hit a grounder to Murphy, who charged in, but the ball went under his glove, allowing Ben Zobrist to score the tying run. Moustakas followed with a single to right field past a diving Murphy, scoring Cain for the go-ahead run.

One night later, before his first pitch in Game Five, Volquez wrote his father's initials behind the mound, and then with a heavy heart, threw six innings of two-run ball.

"He was everything for me," Volquez said of his father. "He was one of the greatest men. I remember he bought me my first glove and my first spikes, brought me to the field. He knew that's what I wanted to be. I wanted to be a baseball player, and he gave me a lot of support."

"For him to pitch the way that he pitched, and get us through six innings, it was a phenomenal performance by him," Yost said of Volquez's effort in Game Five.

The victory marked the eighth comeback win of the postseason for the Royals, who rallied in each of their four wins in the World Series. Perez hit .364 and was named MVP. The year before, he made the final out in Game Seven and watched the San Francisco Giants celebrate on the field the Royals call home. But that was quickly a distant memory.

"I already forget about last year," Perez said minutes after being awarded a red Chevrolet Camaro for being named MVP. "So I just enjoy the moment now. In 2015, Kansas City is No. 1."

A Royal Ball

On November 3, 2015, the Royals showed the might of their new reign. An estimated 800,000 fans crammed into downtown Kansas City for a scene that showed the true sincerity of what the Royals mean to them.

"I told my wife, our fans gave us the greatest gift they could give us today, and that's a lifelong memory of how special they are, and how special this accomplishment is to them," Royals manager Ned Yost said.

Dressed in shirts that read, "Thanks Kansas City," Royals players and coaches watched as families rejoiced in gratitude, a heartfelt thanks for finishing the job. Royals Hall of Famer George Brett rode in on a convertible with a giant foam finger. When he took the stage wearing a blue K.C. cap, he spoke of the 2015 team's place in history.

"I was very, very fortunate to play on so many great Royals teams in my career," Brett said. "I played on the '85 world championship team, and I've followed these guys in spring training forever. But after watching these guys the last two years, I want to thank them for two things: winning the World Series in 2015, and becoming the greatest *team* in Kansas City Royals history. These guys are the best *team* ever!"

Brett, of course, received glorious cheers. But the greatest Royal of them all was actually upstaged by veteran outfielder Jonny Gomes. He was acquired from Atlanta in August and did not make any of the playoff rosters. But Gomes had a few advantages Brett did not during the celebration: an American flag and plenty of liquid courage.

At first, Gomes asked for a moment of silence to honor Mike Moustakas's mom, and the fathers of Chris Young and Edinson Volquez. Then Gomes spoke, somewhat eloquently.

"It's unbelievable what those boys did!" Gomes shouted into the microphone as fans cheered. "It's unbelievable what they did! It's unbelievable what they did! They stole bases, they hit homers. Hey, guess what. Cy Young winner? Not on our

Kansas City Royals manager Ned Yost holds up the Commissioners Trophy for fans during the team's World Series parade route on November 3, 2015, at Union Station in Kansas City, Missouri. (Courtesy *USA TODAY Sports/Denny Medley*)

team, beat him. Rookie of the year? Not on our team, we beat him. MVP of the whole league? Sorry, guys, not on our team. But we beat that guy, too!

"You know why we beat them? Because all of you all people had our backs. And Dayton Moore put this team together and Yost delivered it by being the captain of the ship. You all want to be politically correct? I'm the un-politically correct person. We whooped their ass!"

At that point, Gomes dropped the microphone and was swallowed up on stage in a mosh pit of cheering Royals players. After it calmed down, Alex Gordon, the face of the franchise and a pending free agent at the time, then took the microphone. Under a stocking hat and sun glasses, he looked ahead at the thousands who cheered.

"You guys are the best fans in the world," Gordon said.

But the party, of course, would not have been possible if not for Gordon. His game-tying home run in the bottom of the ninth in Game One put the Royals in control from that moment on. With his future with the club still in doubt, Gordon spoke of all the hardships he faced as a young player, back when the kingdom was being rebuilt.

He also remembered the more recent past, when Game Three starter Noah Syndergaard promised a surprise for the Royals. But it was the Royals who got the ultimate payback.

"All I've got to say is we had a trick up our sleeves, too," Gordon said. "And that's World Series champs."

Fans celebrate as Royals players and team officials ride in the back of pickup trucks during the World Series victory parade in Kansas City. An estimated 800,000 fans came out to celebrate the team's first title since 1985. (Courtesy *Dani Dresslar*)

13
The Future Is Now

A Loyal Royal

The Royals typically aren't big spenders in free agency. But this isn't the same old Royals. They proved that with a World Series title in 2015, and they proved it again on January 6, 2016, when they re-signed Alex Gordon to a four-year deal worth $72 million, which was the largest contract in franchise history, making it a very Happy New Year for Gordon and Royals fans everywhere.

"I just want to say my family and I are very excited and happy to be back in Kansas City," Gordon said during a news conference at Kauffman Stadium announcing the deal. "We've been here for ten years and have kind of established our home here. Coming into the offseason, we were very appreciative of all the teams that showed interest, but at the end of the day my heart has been, and I think always will be in Kansas City."

When free agency began, the likelihood of a reunion between Gordon and the Royals seemed improbable. Shortly after Gordon helped lead the team to the 2015 World Series title, he declined his $14 million player option and later declined the team's $15.8 million qualifying offer to become a free agent.

Royals left fielder Alex Gordon doesn't show a lot of emotion on the baseball field, but he couldn't help it after hitting this game-tying solo home run against the New York Mets in the bottom of the ninth inning in Game One of the 2015 World Series in Kansas City, Missouri. The homer turned the tide for the Royals, who went on to win the title in five games. Gordon later gave Royals fans something else to cheer about that offseason when he signed a four-year contract extension to remain with the team. (Courtesy *USA TODAY Sports/Jeff Curry*)

Before Gordon went down with a severe groin strain in June 2015, many believed he could get a contract of $100 million or more on the open market. But that never materialized, though Gordon did have interest from the Cardinals, Giants, Orioles, and White Sox.

"We were patient about it," Gordon said of his contract. "And my desire was probably a ten to come back here. When I walked in the locker room, it just put a smile on my face because at the end of the season I didn't know if I was going to be able to do that again. Today was definitely a special day."

Gordon's deal surpassed a pair of five-year, $55 million contracts the team handed out to Mike Sweeney and Gil Meche for the biggest in team history.

"At a time within our industry, where it's very challenging for our markets to be able to sign and keep a group of players together—impact talent, which Alex is and made himself a star in this game—and to keep him here in Kansas City obviously is a great honor," Royals general manager Dayton Moore said.

Gordon ranks in the team's top 10 in nearly every offensive category, and he has won four Gold Gloves in left field, ensuring he will be in the team's Hall of Fame someday. He also very well could have his No. 4 retired.

Gordon's career with the Royals began when he was selected second overall in the 2005 draft as a third baseman out of Nebraska. Gordon grew up in Lincoln and rooted for the Royals as a kid. During the summer, his family would make weekend trips to Kauffman Stadium and World of Fun. He would sit in the upper deck and watch his favorite player, George Brett, and dream of being just like him.

Gordon spent the 2006 season playing in Double-A Wichita for manager Frank White and made his MLB debut on Opening Day in 2007. Gordon was billed as the next Brett, but poor play and injuries slowed his development. In 2009, Gordon had surgery to repair a torn labrum in his right hip and missed

Alex Gordon struggled early in his career playing third base but later found a home in left field. Here he is making a running catch against the Baltimore Orioles in Game Four of the 2014 ALCS at Kauffman Stadium. (Courtesy *USA TODAY Sports/Peter G. Aiken*)

about three months. On May 2, 2010, Gordon's struggles were so great that he was sent down to Triple-A Omaha. He also moved to left field, while Mike Moustakas was on the way at third base.

At that point in the season, Gordon was hitting just .194, had already committed four errors, and was labeled another first-round bust. But Gordon's career took off after that, and he became the best left fielder in baseball and an All-Star.

"He's an easy player to root for," Moore said. "He's a great husband, he's a great father, he's a great teammate, and he represents the game of baseball so well. And I've said many times, Alex is one of the greatest player stories I've ever been around in the game. And how he persevered, and how he broke into the major leagues, and the changes he made, and the way he did it, and the way he led, and he didn't complain, he just went to work.

"He is the pillar of our clubhouse and our organization without a doubt, and that's why it was so crucial for us to commit this winter and figure out a way to get him back."

Gordon's teammates also were thrilled to have their leader back, most notably Salvador Perez.

"I wanted that," Perez said. "I feel happy for Gordon and his family. Kansas City, too. And the organization, everyone. He deserved that. He plays hard and plays hurt. He plays 162 games, works hard. He deserves that. Good for him."

Gordon wasn't the only Royal the team re-signed in the offseason. They spent lavishly by re-signing Wade Davis, Alcides Escobar, Lorenzo Cain, Eric Hosmer, Moustakas, and Chris Young. They also brought back former All-Star closer Joakim Soria and spent $70 million on pitcher Ian Kennedy.

In spring training, the Royals made headlines again when they reworked Perez's contract and rewarded him with five years and $52.5 million, showing their fans that they are committed to winning year after year.

Touch of Gold

Opening Day is a celebration usually confined to one day. But when you think about it, what's the harm in having two days of fun? The Royals opened defense of their World Series title on Opening Night, April 3, 2016, with two days of festivities commemorating the team's first championship in thirty years. And in a scheduling quirk, they were part of history once again.

The Royals began their 2016 season with a two-game series at home against the New York Mets, marking the first time in MLB history the two World Series teams from the previous season met on Opening Day. And not only that, but Edinson

Volquez squared off against Matt Harvey, making it the first time in history the two starting pitchers from the deciding game of the World Series met in the season opener the following year.

Wearing specially designed uniforms with "Royals" across their chest in gold lettering, the Royals won 4-3 in front of 40,030 fans, as Volquez threw six scoreless innings and struck out five, using his Game Five World Series glove. During spring training, Volquez said he didn't want to pitch the first game of the season because he enjoyed watching the pregame ceremony as a fan. But he changed his mind after his first Opening Day start at The K.

"It's unbelievable, especially pitching at home here where they love the team and they love every single player on the whole team," Volquez said after the win. "It was great to win the first game in front of those people."

Volquez's only miscue of the night was when he put on the wrong hat. He pitched the first inning wearing a Royals spring training hat instead of the specially designed hat they were supposed to wear for the opener.

"They put two in my locker, and I grabbed the first one," Volquez said.

The umpires didn't say anything to Volquez before the game, but Salvador Perez noticed, and when Volquez got to the dugout, he was informed he was wearing the wrong hat.

"That was funny," Perez said with a laugh. "I told him, throw a one-two-three inning and you can go back out with the same hat. He can wear any hat he wants."

Not quite. The MLB rulebook says players must wear matching uniforms at all times and any player who does not adhere to that can't play in the game. So technically, Volquez was in violation of baseball's dress code, but he was not fined.

When Volquez came back out for the second inning, he took the field with the right hat on. The spring training hat that he initially wore was then sold during the game as a special game-used item at the Royals' team store.

Two days later, the Royals received their 2015 World Series championship rings in a special pregame ceremony. For Royals manager Ned Yost, it was the second time he was awarded a World Series championship ring, having won his first as a coach with Atlanta in 1995.

"I'll wear it for it while," Yost said. "I found myself many times last year just staring at our American League championship ring, just how great it was to get back to the playoffs, and the excitement that it brought to our city, and I'll do that with this ring. I'll look at it and sit there and stare at it and think how great an accomplishment it is."

Mike Moustakas initially wasn't sure if he would wear his ring right away, but he and some of his teammates already had quite a collection.

"Coming up through the minor leagues in the organization, we won a ton of rings in Double-A and Triple-A," Moustakas said. "But this is a little more special than all of those. I'm not sure if I'll wear it (right away), but I will at some point. It's something special that I want to keep for a long time.

"This is what you play the game for. It's something you look forward to your entire life, making a World Series. And to actually win one is a pretty special feeling."

The Wizard of Hoz

In 2015, Eric Hosmer had All-Star numbers, but he didn't get to join his Royal teammates in Cincinnati. But on July 12, 2016, Hosmer was the AL's starting first baseman for the All-Star Game in San Diego, and the left-handed hitting slugger had a night he likely won't forget.

Hosmer, who entered play hitting .299 with 13 homers and 49 RBIs, was named MVP after getting two hits, including a home run, to go with two RBIs in the AL's 4-2 win over the NL. Hosmer became the first Royal since Bo Jackson in 1989 to be named MVP of the Midsummer Classic.

"It's a great feeling," Hosmer said after the game. "It's extremely humbling. Honestly, I was just so happy to be a part of all this, and to be part of the team and make the All-Star Game for the first time. I never thought about becoming the MVP. I just wanted to soak up the whole experience, and it's everything and more you could ever ask for."

In his first All-Star at-bat in the second inning, Hosmer faced friend-turned-foe Johnny Cueto of the San Francisco Giants. On a 1-1 count, Hosmer hit a 90 mph cutter 389 feet to left field for a homer. It also was the first time a Royal had homered in the All-Star Game since Jackson in '89.

Shortly after Hosmer's blast, Salvador Perez hit a two-run homer to left to give the AL a 3-1 lead, making Hosmer and Perez the eighth pair of teammates to homer in the same All-Star Game.

"It was really cool," Hosmer said. "I was getting ready to do an interview with Ken Rosenthal, and he was telling me I was the first one to hit one since Bo, and we both look up and see Salvy hit one. Couldn't have worked out any better. Salvy and I go way back. A lot of you guys know we have been playing this game together for a long time, and to share that experience and have the games we did, tonight was really special."

It also was special for Royals manager Ned Yost.

Eric Hosmer of the Kansas City Royals was named the MVP of the 2016 MLB All Star Game at Petco Park in San Diego. Hosmer had a home run and two RBIs in his first appearance in the Midsummer Classic. (Courtesy *USA TODAY Sports/Gary A. Vasquez*)

"I was so proud of Hoz when he hit that ball, and Salvy when he hit it," said Yost, who managed in his second straight All-Star Game. "I felt like a proud papa."

For being named MVP, Hosmer also received a brand new black Chevy Colorado, which he gave to his father, Mike, a retired firefighter. Why the generous gift?

"So he can stop stealing all of my cars," Hosmer joked.

The All-Star Game marked another chapter in Hosmer's brief but storied career. He has experienced the ultimate highs and lows as a ballplayer for the Royals. He's gone from prized prospect to bust to World Series champion to All-Star MVP and one of the best young hitters in the game. His defense also has been stellar at times, earning three Gold Gloves.

"We believed in him from the time we drafted him in high school," Royals general manager Dayton Moore said. "And he's done nothing along his career path to allow us to feel any different about him. He's a special talent. He loves to play the game, and he's a great teammate, and he's outstanding with the fans and the community. He can beat you on both sides of the ball."

While Hosmer's career is still trending upward, so is his popularity. A few months before the All-Star Game, Hosmer and several teammates went to the Justin Bieber concert at the Sprint Center in Kansas City. As Hosmer was leaving the arena, he was mobbed by fans. Trying to free himself from the massive crowd, he noticed a young girl had fallen while trying to reach him.

The crowd, however, did not stop, possibly putting the girl in harm's way. So Hosmer cleared space and helped the girl up before something happened, a gesture that earned him more kudos with the fans. But when asked if ever thought of himself as the most popular athlete in Kansas City, Hosmer just shrugged.

"I don't know," Hosmer said. "I just try to come in and be a baseball player, and obviously it was pretty crazy what happened. The people here in Kansas City have treated me well my whole entire career through positives and negatives. So I'm just really appreciative of it all. I guess that's what happens when you win a world championship."

Perez, a popular player himself, knows what Hosmer is going through and said it's easy to see why Hosmer connects with the fans so strongly.

"It's his personality," Perez said. "He's the best. He cares about the fans, he cares about the players and the team. He's got a good personality."

And a powerful bat. In 2016, Hosmer finished with a career-high 25 home runs and a career-high 104 RBIs. He also was named the team's Player of the Year.

Welcome to the White House

The East Room of the White House is a unique place. The largest room in the Executive Mansion, it is used for receptions, press conferences, meetings with world leaders, and other special events.

One such event took place July 21, 2016, when President Barack Obama honored the 2015 World Series champions. As the Royals took the stage in the room with gold curtains, chandeliers, and high ceilings, they heard a familiar sound. It's a sound that has traveled with them to San Francisco, Texas, Toronto, and New York, and everywhere in between.

Barack Obama, the forty-fourth President of the United States, poses with a Kansas City Royals jersey during a ceremony honoring the 2015 World Series champs at the White House on July 21, 2016. (Courtesy *REUTERS/Carlos Barria*)

"Let's go, Royals!"

The chant started small but grew louder and louder. Obama entered the room flanked by Royals owner David Glass and team president Dan Glass. At the podium, Obama linked the past to the present.

"Let's give it up for the World Series champions, the Kansas City Royals," Obama said, evoking cheers from the crowd. "I know many of you have been waiting a long time to hear this, so I'll say it again—the World Series champion Kansas City Royals!"

The crowd cheered again before Obama took a minute to retrace the franchise's struggles following the team's World Series title in 1985.

"Let's face it, it's been a long road for Royals fans," Obama said. "There were some dark years, some tough decades."

Obama acknowledged that the team's turnaround began when Dayton Moore was hired in 2006, and the franchise took a pivotal turn for the better when Ned Yost became manager in 2010. To fix baseball's biggest disaster, Moore "coupled some of baseball's sharpest analytics minds with Ned's managerial style, which has produced a lot of wins," Obama said. "Not to mention his own Twitter hashtag—hashtag Yosted."

The crowd laughed, harkening back to a time when Yost was one of the most despised people in Kansas City. Obama then praised homegrown players Alex "Gordo" Gordon, Mike "Moose" Moustakas, Eric "Hoz" Hosmer, and Salvador "Salvy" Perez, before joking about their nicknames.

"These guys are all great players. Can I say, though, the nicknames aren't that creative," Obama said, once again getting laughs from the crowd and the team. "It's like, Barack 'Barack' Obama. You know? I mean, listen to this. Hoz, Moose, Gordo. We're going to have to work on these."

Obama mentioned the team's outstanding bullpen led by Wade Davis and Kelvin Herrera, and the team's defense and speed, pausing to look at outfielder Jarrod Dyson.

"'That's what speed do.' That was a good quote," Obama said, referring to the phrase the speedy Dyson coined a few years back.

The ceremony was brief, lasting only about fifteen minutes. But in that time, Obama also spoke of the team's fan support, which was evident in the All-Star voting and especially early when it looked like the entire infield would be Royals because fans stuffed the online ballot box.

"As a Chicago guy, I appreciate that," Obama said jokingly. "Vote early, vote often."

Obama also mentioned the Royals' new Urban Youth Academy in Kansas City, which is spearheaded by Moore, and how their playoff run in 2014 set the stage for 2015, which culminated in their second championship.

"I want to thank this group for not only writing the current chapter, but hopefully writing the next chapter of our national pastime, the great game of baseball," Obama said in his closing remarks before Yost handed Obama a Royals World Series championship jersey with gold lettering and the No. 44 on it.

During their trip to the White House, teammates posed together for pictures, with Perez and Hosmer striking a pose in front of a portrait of Abraham Lincoln. After they were done in D.C., the Royals boarded a plane bound for Kansas City and returned home.

"That was a great," Perez said. "It was a neat experience and not too many people get the opportunity to shake hands with the president. We had a great time. We got to see the White House, and the tour was a lot of fun."

It was a glorious day, indeed. But Perez wished he could have given Obama a Royal welcome of his own, complete with a Gatorade bucket and a Salvy Splash.

"I wanted to do it," Perez said with a big laugh. "But people told me not to so I didn't do it."

But a Salvy Splash isn't necessarily out of the question permanently. When asked if he would consider doing it in the future should he return to the White House again, Perez just smiled and laughed.

"You never know," Perez said.

Duffy Becomes Dominant

It's a beautiful Sunday morning in late September 2016. In about three hours the Royals will play the White Sox at Kauffman Stadium. As I'm driving north to the ballpark on a stretch of I-435, there's a black Cadillac Escalade ahead in the distance.

In the left-hand lane, I gain ground on the SUV that is in the middle lane and slowed behind traffic. As I go to pass, I see something out of the corner of my eye. From my vantage point, the SUV is getting a bit too close to the right side of my car.

My eyes widen, and I quickly look over. The driver of the Escalade has his hat on backward and a clean-shaven beard. The driver also is wearing a big smile and waving as if he recognized me. He did. I also recognized the driver: Danny Duffy.

When Duffy later spotted me in the clubhouse before the game, we both laughed. Duffy also just happened to be the team's starting pitcher that day, and he went out and threw seven quality innings in a 10-3 Royals win.

I share this story for two reasons: one, because it's just so cool, and two, because that's Danny Duffy, the genuine fun-loving kid who once tweeted "bury me a Royal" after signing a contract in 2012 and later evolving into the Royals ace.

Duffy's rise to prominence can be traced back to a cool fall day in 2015, when he played catch with Kris Medlen in the outfield at Kauffman Stadium. While the Royals were charging toward a World Series title, an experiment was taking place as Duffy gripped the baseball in his hand searching for a new breaking ball.

"I was just messing around tinkering with it," Duffy said.

Duffy gripped the ball like a fastball and fired. When Medlen caught the ball, he was mesmerized by what is now Duffy's slider.

"Dude, you got to take that into a game," Medlen told him.

When the ball popped into Medlen's glove, Duffy's career was at a crossroads. When the Royals drafted him in the third round of the 2007 draft out of Cabrillo High School in Lompoc, California, they were hoping they had found a left-hander who could be part of the rotation for years. For a while, it looked like they were right as Duffy showed flashes of brilliance before injury, ineffectiveness, and wildness sent him to the bullpen for the 2014 and 2015 playoffs and the start of the 2016 season.

For years, Duffy was a three-pitch pitcher, using a fastball, changeup, and a big curveball. His fastball could hit 98 mph, and his changeup could make a batter twist out of his shoes. But his curveball was hit and miss.

So Duffy dropped the curveball and went and discussed the possibility of throwing the slider in games with Royals pitching coach Dave Eiland. After some refining, including tweaking the grip, Duffy was given the OK.

After performing well out of the bullpen to start the 2016 season, Duffy was reinserted into the rotation when Medlen and Chris Young went down with injuries in May. Turns out, it was the best move Royals manager Ned Yost made all year.

When Duffy rejoined the rotation, the 6-foot-2, 205-pounder finally put it together. At one point, he won ten straight starts, going from the bullpen to putting himself in contention for the Cy Young Award.

"I'm just real proud of him to see the development in him, and how he's turned the corner and just turned into a top-notch pitcher in the American League," Yost said.

Duffy's best outing came on August 1 at Tampa Bay when he took a no-hitter into the eighth and struck out a team record sixteen batters in one game, surpassing Zack Greinke's mark of fifteen in 2009. Against the Rays, it was one of those rare nights when a starting pitcher has all three pitches working. His fastball was jumping out of his hand, his changeup was really good, and his slider was on. Duffy even got the Rays to swing and miss an astonishing thirty-five times. The Royals won 3-0, and Duffy received two Salvy Splashes afterward.

"I had to," Perez said.

Duffy has always been a fan favorite, but there were some trying times before he got to the big leagues. In March 2010, the likable lefty walked away from the game to "reassess his life priorities." He went home to Lompoc, a small town of about 42,000 an hour away from Santa Barbara.

"We got like five hotels, a penitentiary, and missile launching pads, and an Air Force Base," Duffy said.

While at his parents' house, Duffy realized how much he missed the game. He returned to the team three months later before making his MLB debut in May 2011. When Duffy underwent Tommy John surgery a year later, he again returned home to recover, spending time running along the beach when his mind needed a respite.

Kansas City Royals left-hander Danny Duffy pitches against the New York Mets on June 22, 2016, at Citi Field in New York. Duffy began the season out of the bullpen but quickly became the team's top starter. (Courtesy *USA TODAY Sports/Brad Penner*)

After the 2014 World Series, Duffy stopped his offseason regimen of running and instead focused on gaining weight and building his core. He also said he "didn't watch a single highlight" of baseball that offseason.

But in the offseason following the 2015 World Series, Duffy said he watched Wade Davis's last pitch against the Mets "500 times." Sure, Duffy watched it to celebrate and cherish the team's World Series title, but it also was a motivational tactic to fuel his desire to get there again.

So to begin the offseason, Duffy hit the road, running again, and it paid off. And pitching exclusively out of the stretch, Duffy had far better command and finished the season 12-3 with a 3.51 ERA. He struck out 188 and walked just 42 in 179 ⅔ innings. Opponents hit just .241 against him.

Obviously, Duffy has plenty of talent, but how much credit goes to the famous bear suit he keeps in the clubhouse?

"Zero at all," he said with a laugh.

True enough, as Duffy no doubt deserves the credit for his best season in the big leagues. Despite Duffy's season, and the luck of a rally mantis, the Royals finished the 2016 season 81-81 and missed the playoffs for the first time in three years. Duffy, though, was named the team's Pitcher of the Year, and in the offseason he signed a five-year, $65 million contract to stay in Kansas City.

"I wouldn't have it any other way," Duffy said.

At the time of the Duffy signing, the Royals had their top two starters signed to long-term contracts. But tragedy would strike just days later, altering the course of 2017 and beyond.

"We Loved Yordano"

Yordano Ventura had the stuff legends were made of—a 102 mph fastball, a devastating curveball, and a changeup he could throw five times in a row for strikes. His talent was rare and his future so bright.

But on January 22, 2017, Ventura died in a car accident in his native Dominican Republic. Ventura—gone too soon at age twenty-five—was the first player in team history to die while being on the active roster.

As news of Ventura's death reached the United States, his teammates were going about their normal Sunday routines. Drew Butera had just gone to church with his dad. Christian Colon was spending time with his family in Kansas City, and Mike Moustakas was in bed in California.

Royals manager Ned Yost was on his farm, and general manager Dayton Moore was on his way to the airport to catch a plane headed to Atlanta when he received a call from Major League Baseball confirming Ventura had died. Early that afternoon, on a somber conference call with the media, Moore reminisced about Ventura, the kid who dropped out of school at age fourteen and worked construction to help support his family but grew up to become a beloved ballplayer for the Royals.

"We loved Yordano," Moore said. "We loved his heart, he was a teammate, a friend."

Ventura was born on June 3, 1991, in Samana, Dominican Republic. The Royals discovered him at a tryout camp and signed him when he was just seventeen. Nicknamed "Ace" for his power and potential, Ventura made it to the big leagues

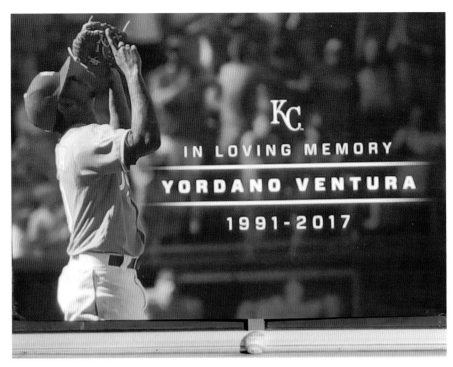

A sign memorializing Royals pitcher Yordano Ventura was put up outside Kauffman Stadium after he died in his native Dominican Republic on January 22, 2017. (Courtesy *Jess Coffey*)

on September 17, 2013. In 2014, Ventura went 14-10 and had a 3.20 ERA and took sixth in the AL Rookie of the Year voting.

In parts of four seasons with the Royals, Ventura had a career record of 38-31 in 94 games (93 starts). Ventura, who was an emotional player on the field, is probably best remembered for his performance in Game Six of the 2014 World Series against San Francisco when he pitched seven shutout innings and fanned four in the 10-0 Royals win.

For that start, Ventura honored his late friend Oscar Taveras, an outfielder for the St. Louis Cardinals who had died just days earlier in a car accident in the Dominican. On his Royals cap, Ventura wrote: "RIP OT #18."

After learning of Ventura's death, a memorial was set up at Kauffman Stadium where fans brought flowers, cards, signs, jerseys, and hats. Flags also were lowered to half-mast. As mourners grieved at the stadium, two of Ventura's teammates, Christian Colon and Danny Duffy, stopped by and offered fans their condolences.

Later that night, a candlelight vigil was held at the stadium. Colon, Duffy, and Ian Kennedy were among the Royals in attendance.

"I didn't really know what to do," Colon said. "We just went and hugged anybody that wanted a hug, and Danny and I probably needed a hug and [time] to process what happened, and it seemed like the field was the right place to be.

"I loved it so much the first time, we went back at night, and it was even bigger, and the fans were there supporting us. They've done a tremendous job being there for us."

Several members of the organization, including Yost, Moore, Moustakas, Eric Hosmer, Salvador Perez, and Alcides Escobar, traveled to the Dominican for Ventura's funeral. Perez even gave a eulogy at the pitcher's mound where Ventura played as a kid.

Back home less than a week later at the team's annual FanFest in Kansas City, the Royals honored Ventura with a memorial that featured a pitcher's mound with his No. 30, a game-worn Ventura jersey, pictures, video highlights, and a signature wall.

For Colon, who served as Ventura's interpreter many times in interviews, his hand-written-message was short and sweet: "Yo, you'll always be my brother. I'll always love you. Rest in peace."

The loss of Ventura leaves a huge hole for the Royals on a personal level and the baseball side. The Royals had signed him to a five-year, $23 million deal in 2015 with two option years that could have kept him in Kansas City through the 2021 season. And replacing the baseball side of it is the easy part.

"When you reflect about Yordano, it's not what you miss on the baseball field," Yost said. "It's the relationship that you're going to miss, it's the friendship, his smile in the locker room, his laugh, and him walking in every day and saying, 'Hey, Ned Yo!' Those are the things you miss. You don't even think about what his contributions were going to be on the baseball field."

But baseball is back. And the Royals are honoring Ventura in 2017 with an "Ace 30" patch on the right sleeve of their uniform. They also are moving forward.

"I think that's the way Yordano would want it in the first place is for us to strap it on and get ready to go," Hosmer said. "It's up to us to live out his legacy now."

The Royals have several new faces for the 2017 season. Edinson Volquez signed as a free agent with the Marlins, Kendrys Morales signed with the Blue Jays, Wade Davis was traded to the Cubs for outfielder Jorge Soler, and Jarrod Dyson was traded to the Mariners for pitcher Nathan Karns.

The Royals also signed veteran slugger Brandon Moss to shore up the lineup and added veteran Jason Hammel to help replace Ventura in the rotation. And

The Royals honored pitcher Yordano Ventura with another memorial at the team's FanFest in January 2017 at Bartle Hall in Kansas City, Missouri. (Courtesy *Jeff Deters*)

with the core group still largely intact for 2017, the Royals could be World Series contenders once again.

From $5.3 million to start the franchise to World Series champs, and from doormats to reclaiming the crown, the Royals' story is far from finished, but no doubt one that will continue to amaze.

A Note on Sources

Some of the information and quotes used in *Miracle Moments in Kansas City Royals History* came from the author's years of covering the team beginning in 2013. That included interviews with: Willie Aikens, Steve Balboni, Carlos Beltran, Buddy Biancalana, George Brett, Steve Busby, Drew Butera, Billy Butler, Lorenzo Cain, Bruce Chen, Christian Colon, David Cone, Johnny Cueto, Cheslor Cuthbert, Wade Davis, Danny Duffy, Jarrod Dyson, Alcides Escobar, Al Fitzmorris, David Glass, Jonny Gomes, Alex Gordon, Terrance Gore, Mark Gubicza, Jeremy Guthrie, Ed Hearn, Kelvin Herrera, Whitey Herzog, Luke Hochevar, Greg Holland, Eric Hosmer, Jana Howser, Mike Jirschele, Julia Irene Kauffman, Ian Kennedy, Rusty Kuntz, Dennis Leonard, Buck Martinez, Denny Matthews, Brian McRae, Kris Medlen, Raul Mondesi, Dayton Moore, Kendrys Morales, Mike Moustakas, Paulo Orlando, Amos Otis, Salvador Perez, Greg Pryor, Janie Quisenberry-Stone, Alex Rios, Bret Saberhagen, Ervin Santana, Kevin Seitzer, James Shields, Joakim Soria, Art Stewart, Mike Sweeney, Pat Tabler, Yordano Ventura, Edinson Volquez, Frank White, Ned Yost, Chris Young, Ben Zobrist, and more.

References

Books:

Black, Del, Bordman, Sid, Sands, Bob, Henderson, Joe and Murray, Jim, *From Worst . . . to First: A History of Kansas City Major League Baseball 1955-85*. 2016.

Bondy, Filip, *The Pine Tar Game: The Kansas City Royals, The New York Yankees, and Baseball's Most Absurd and Entertaining Controversy*. Scribner, 2015.

Gorman, Lou, *High and Inside: My Life in the Front Offices of Baseball*. McFarland, 2007.

Gretz, Bob, *Tales from the Kansas City Chiefs Sideline*. Sports Publishing, 2015.

Moore, Dayton and Fulks, Matt, *More Than a Season: Building a Championship Culture*. Triumph Books, 2015, 2016.

Quisenberry, Dan, *On Days Like This: Poems*. Helicon Nine Editions, 1998.

White, Frank and Althaus, Bill, *One Man's Dream: My Town, My Team, My Time*. Ascend Books, 2012.

Newspaper and Wire Services:

Associated Press, *Baltimore Sun, Chicago Tribune, Kansas City Star, Los Angeles Times, Topeka Capital-Journal, New York Times, Orlando Sentinel, St. Louis Post Dispatch, Wall Street Journal, Washington Post.*

Websites:

Baseball-almanac.com, baseball-refernce.com, CBSsports.com, ESPN.com, joeposnanski.com, kansas.city.royals.mlb.com, www.kauffman.org, mlb.com, pro-football-reference.com, royalsreview.com, SI.com.